SPIRALISE!

SPIRALISE!

60 delicious meals to make
with your spiraliser

PETE EVANS

CONTENTS

INTRODUCTION

G'day friends. Thank you for making an investment in your health by buying this book of delicious spiraliser recipes. I love my spiraliser and use it to create all kinds of different meals. This brilliant invention is changing the way we cook and eat, allowing us to include more vegetables in our diet in creative ways. Spiralisers are perfect for busy families, as they are so quick and easy to use. And they're an excellent way to encourage your kids to eat veggies – they will find it fascinating seeing a perfect vegetable getting pushed and turned like a pencil on a sharpener into long, curly ribbons or noodles. Spiralisers also make sense as part of a paleo lifestyle, and can be helpful for people who are making the transition to this way of living.

So, why is the spiraliser a perfect fit with a paleo lifestyle? Well, paleo is about embracing an abundance of vegetables, and a spiraliser is a great way to do this. You can use a wide range of vegetables in your spiraliser, and they are delicious both raw and cooked. You can also ferment spiralised veggies (see recipes on pages 58, 60 and 63) – they taste and look amazing! I always include a tablespoon or two of fermented vegetables with every meal for good gut health, and the spiraliser has opened up new ways to play around with fermented veg. Another way to promote good gut health is by incorporating bone broth into your diet. I love to sauté and blanch my spiralised veggies in bone broth to maximise the nutritional benefits, or simply pop some spirals into a bowl of warm bone broth to start your day in the best way possible.

Paleo is also about eliminating refined sugars and potentially inflammatory foods, such as grains and dairy, from our diet. Pasta, noodles, rice and bread are some of the most common dishes that are hard for people to give up. Here, again, the spiraliser can really help, as you can use it to replace noodles, pasta and other grain-based dishes with something that is 100 times more nutrient dense – veggie noodles and pasta!

Spiralised veggies are versatile and can be incorporated into all kinds of meals. As part of a paleo lifestyle, I try to include a palm-sized piece of high-quality protein with most meals, and there's nothing better to go alongside this than a colourful, spiralised raw veggie salad. Add some good-quality natural fat from avocados, olives, coconuts, nuts, seeds, eggs or animals and you're pretty much covering all nutritional bases.

For me, there's no choice between a bowl of traditional spaghetti bolognese and one with veggie noodles instead of pasta. The first option makes me feel bloated and heavy, while the second is far more nutritionally dense, easier to digest and leaves me feeling satisfied and full of energy. I reckon bolognese with veggie noodles also wins in the taste department! Here's my logic. If I cooked you up a plate of pasta with no sauce on it, you would probably find it pretty bland. However, if I served you up a bowl of sautéed zucchini, carrot and pumpkin noodles, you would surely agree it has a lot more flavour. So it makes sense that if you top both with a delicious sauce, the vegetable noodle bowl will taste better than the pasta one!

To help you get started on this spiralising journey, I've included a guide to the basics of spiralising (see pages 8–11). Different brands of spiralisers will vary slightly, so make sure you read the manufacturer's instructions carefully and learn about the different parts before you begin. While spiralisers are generally very safe to use, the blades are sharp so be careful and make sure you supervise your children if they want to get involved.

I've also included a guide to some of my favourite vegetables and fruits to spiralise (see pages 12–19). Some are easier to spiralise than others, but just have a go and see what you enjoy the most. Finally, I've shared more than 60 simple dishes that are packed full of flavour and feature loads of vibrant spiralised veggies. You'll be amazed at the huge range of ways spirals can add interest, colour and texture to all kinds of dishes, from fresh salads to warming soups, spicy curries, stir-fries and roasts.

I love this way of eating, and I'm sure you are going to love it too. Once you get in the swing of using spiralised vegetables, you'll see just how easy and fun it can be – especially if you get the kids involved! Think of your spiraliser as a new way to treat yourself and your family to the most nutritious food on the planet. Now, it's time to get cooking (and spiralising!) with love and laughter for good health.

Pete Evans

SPIRALISING BASICS

GETTING STARTED

Congratulations on embarking on a new culinary adventure with your spiraliser! This cool gadget is a great addition to a healthy lifestyle, helping you and your family to get more delicious veggies onto your plate every day. Spiralisers are simple to both use and clean, inexpensive, and small enough to be easily stored.

Spiralisers have actually been around for many years and were originally a Japanese invention. It's only in the last few years that they have become more widely used, and there are now heaps of brands on the market. While they may vary in size, shape and blade types, they all tend to do the same job and give similar results.

Before you start spiralising, make sure you read through the manufacturer's instructions to get to know the ins and outs of your particular brand. While spiralisers are generally really safe to use, always use them with care, and keep in mind that the blades are razor sharp. Your kids will probably love to help, just make sure you supervise them carefully.

WHAT KINDS OF VEGETABLES AND FRUITS CAN I SPIRALISE?

I have tested loads of different vegetables and fruits in the spiraliser, and the good news is there are heaps that work beautifully (see pages 12–19 for details on specific veggies and fruits).

Generally, spiralising works best for medium- and hard-fleshed vegetables and fruits, such as zucchini, carrot, beetroot, parsnip, turnip, sweet potato and apple. Softer produce such as eggplants, tomatoes, ripe pears and stone fruits will generally turn to mush if you try to put them through the spiraliser, so it's best to avoid them. Celery, leek, capsicum and other vegetables without a solid centre don't work well either, so I recommend sticking with a regular kitchen knife for these veggies.

You can also use your spiraliser for thinly slicing onions, shredding cabbage or making sweet potato fries. You'll save so much time doing it this way rather than by slicing or shredding by hand!

HOW DO I USE MY SPIRALISER?

Spiralisers do vary slightly from brand to brand, so it's important to experiment with your own device to see what works best. However, there are still some overall steps that can be followed with pretty much any spiraliser, so here are the basics to get you started.

STEP 1.

Trim both ends off the vegetable so that each end is flat. The pieces need to be evenly shaped throughout, about 5 cm in diameter and no more than 15 cm in length. You may need to cut the vegetable in half if it's larger than 15 cm, or trim it if it's not the right width. (Save the trimmings for broths, soups and sauces.)

STEP 2.

Place your spiraliser on a clean, dry benchtop. Most spiralisers come with suction cup feet, so press the spiraliser firmly down until the suction cup feet are well secured onto the surface. You want the device to stay in place during use. Avoid wooden surfaces, as they may not work well.

STEP 3.

Next, attach the blade size you wish to use by sliding it into the appropriate place indicated on the manufacturer's instructions (see page 11 for a description of the different blades).

STEP 4.

Place one trimmed end of the vegetable into the core blade and slightly press through to insert. Make sure the core blade is positioned through the centre of the vegetable. Move the gripper handle to the other end of the vegetable and push to firmly secure the vegetable into place.

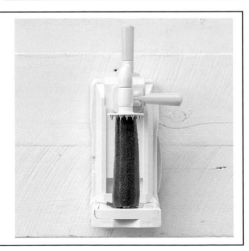

STEP 5.

Use one hand to hold the handle on the bottom side of the spiraliser and place the other hand on the spiraliser's turning handle. Turn in a clockwise direction. The vegetable will be pushed through the blades, creating long curly noodles.

HOW DO I CHOOSE WHICH BLADE TO USE?

Most spiralisers come with 3 interchangeable blades: thin, thick and straight (some also come with an ultra-thin blade). The names of these blades may differ but they all have similar sizes and shapes. Throughout this book, we've specified for veggies and fruits to be spiralised into 'thin noodles', 'thick noodles' or 'ribbons'. Feel free to play around with the blades to choose whichever sized noodle you like best, just keep a close eye when cooking them, as the cooking time will vary depending on the thickness of the noodles.

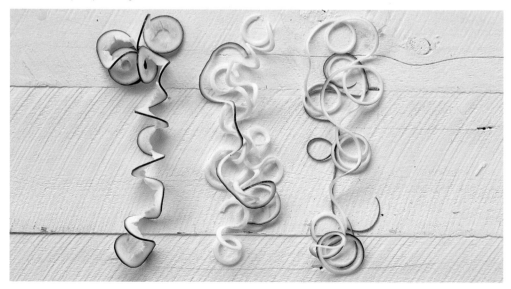

Straight or ribbon blade

The straight or ribbon blade is used to thinly slice vegetables into wide ribbon-shaped noodles. This blade is also used for shredding and is great for slicing cabbage, onions and fennel. You can make sweet potato or parsnip chips using this blade too. Ribbons will take about 1–2 minutes to cook in boiling water or broth, or 2–5 minutes to sauté in a frying pan.

Thin noodle blade

The thin blade produces thin noodle strands, similar in thickness to spaghetti. It will take roughly 30–60 seconds to cook them in boiling water or broth, or about 1–2 minutes to sauté.

Ultra thin blade

Some spiralisers come with a fourth blade to create super thin noodles that resemble angel hair pasta. These are great for salads or to use as a garnish.

Thick noodle blade

The thick blade produces very thick noodle strands. These are great for baked dishes, sweet potato or zucchini fries and stir-fries. Thick veggie noodles will generally take about 1–2 minutes to cook in boiling water or broth, or 3–5 minutes to sauté in a frying pan.

HANDY TIPS & TRICKS

- I like to spiralise a big batch of veggies, pack them in snap-lock bags and store them in the fridge for later use. I find that most vegetables hold pretty well and last a few days when refrigerated. Some vegetables, such as celeriac, daikon, carrot and beetroot, will keep longer stored in water in the fridge (see pages 12–19 for more information on individual vegetables).

- A lot of juice can come out when you spiralise vegetables and fruits, so it's best to keep a kitchen towel handy to clean up the juices when needed.

- If you've got the space, find a spot for your spiraliser on the benchtop so that it's ready for use at any time of day.

- Vegetable and fruit spirals generally don't freeze well, as they become mushy when thawed.

- When spiralising vegetables and fruits, you will be left with a long, round centre core that comes through during the process. Don't throw these out – they are great as a snack for school lunches, or you can chop them up and add them to sauces, soups, salads or roasts.

- If you find that your veggies aren't spiralising properly, or if you're having difficulty gripping the handle when turning, it may be because the vegetable is too large. The vegetable should be no more than 15 cm in length and about 5 cm wide.

SPIRAL TYPES

APPLE

Apples are a beautiful fruit to spiralise because of their lovely firm texture and shape. Make sure you remove the stem from the top and you will need to slice a little bit off two opposite sides so the apple sits nicely on the spiraliser.

It's best to serve apple noodles raw, but if you choose to cook them, you can sauté them in a frying pan with a little oil for 1 minute, or roast them in the oven for 1–2 minutes.

The thick blade and straight/ribbon blade are the best blades to use for apples, but, having said that, you can also use the thin blade, as they all work well. Apple noodles can be used in bircher muesli, salads, slaws, baked dishes and stir-fries.

Store apple noodles in lemon water, as apple tends to oxidise very quickly, in an airtight container in the fridge for up to 1 week.

BEETROOT

Beetroot have a sweet, earthy flavour and are highly nutritious, with potassium, magnesium, fibre, phosphorus, iron, vitamins A, B and C, betacarotene and folic acid. Their beautiful colour makes all kinds of dishes look amazing.

Wear gloves when you're spiralising beetroot, as it will stain your hands. If you're eating the beetroot raw, spiralise it into thin noodles, but for roasting or boiling, thick noodles or ribbons are best. Roasting beetroot is the best method for cooking, as it maintains that earthy, sweet flavour.

Raw beetroot noodles are great for salads, but juice can seep out, turning the whole salad a pinkish colour. To prevent this, fill a bowl with ice-cold water, submerge the beetroot and soak for a couple of minutes, until the beetroot feels nice and crisp. Drain, rinse and dry well.

Raw spiralised beetroot lasts for 4–5 days stored in an airtight container or snap-lock bag in the fridge. To preserve their crisp texture, you can also store beetroot noodles in a container of water in the fridge.

CARROT

Carrots are among the most popular root vegetables all across the world. They are delicious, crunchy and full of flavour and, most importantly, are packed full of nutrients and healthy compounds, such as betacarotene, falcarinol, vitamin A, minerals and antioxidants.

Spiralising carrot is simple to do. It is a firm vegetable and has the perfect shape to sit nicely on a spiraliser. The only thing is to make sure you use large carrots, as small skinny ones can be a little tricky to fit through the spiraliser. You can spiralise to whatever thickness you like and the noodles or ribbons can be eaten raw, cooked, boiled, roasted or fried. Whatever you choose will taste delicious and can be used in salads, stir-fries, curries and bakes.

Store raw carrot noodles in an airtight container or a snap-lock bag in the refrigerator for 3–4 days. To maintain their crisp texture, you can also store them in a container of water in the fridge.

CELERIAC

Celeriac, also known as celery root, is a good source of vitamin K and essential minerals such as phosphorus, iron, calcium, copper and manganese.

Celeriac can be a little difficult to spiralise, mainly because it's heavy and has very firm flesh. Try to use a small celeriac, peel away the skin and cut a little bit off two opposite sides to help it sit nicely on the spiraliser. If the celeriac is quite large, cut it in half crossways and then slice a little off each end, before fitting it on the spiraliser.

When spiralising, use the thick blade. You can roast the celeriac noodles in the oven preheated to 180°C for 5–6 minutes, or until cooked through; blanch them in simmering bone broth or salted water for 1 minute; or sauté them in a little oil or fat in a frying pan over medium heat until al dente. You can also serve celeriac noodles raw – they are a great addition to salads, especially slaws, and sauces, such as remoulades.

Celeriac tends to oxidise, so store the raw noodles in lemon water in an airtight container in the fridge for up to 5 days.

CUCUMBER

Cucumbers are great pick-me-ups, as they are a good source of B vitamins. They have a refreshing flavour and are a good way to rehydrate. They're a wonderful addition to Japanese, Thai or garden salads.

When spiralising cucumbers, try to use large, thick ones and make sure they are firm; soft cucumbers become mushy going through a spiraliser. The best blades are for thin and thick noodles. Slice a little off each end of the cucumber before spiralising.

It's best to spiralise cucumbers just before serving as they quickly become watery.

GREEN PAPAYA

Green papaya is full of essential nutrients and enzymes for heart and gut health. It contains vitamins A, C and E and folate.

Remove the skin and seeds and trim to a roundish or squarish shape so it fits on the spiraliser. Green papaya is best served raw or fermented (see page 60) and is great tossed through salads. Use the thin noodle blade.

Green papaya noodles last for 2–3 days stored in an airtight container or snap-lock bag in the fridge. You can also store them in a container filled with water in the fridge, to maintain crispness.

DAIKON

Daikon, high in vitamin C and folic acid, is a long white vegetable from the radish family. It is delicious raw and adds a crunchy texture to salads. Daikon is also great in soups – just pour the hot broth over the daikon noodles and they will cook nicely while still retaining a slight crunch.

To prepare, wash and peel the daikon and cut off the ends to flatten, then cut in half crossways so it fits on the spiraliser. You can use all blades as it spiralises very easily.

Raw spiralised daikon lasts for 4–5 days stored in an airtight container or snap-lock bag in the fridge. You can also store the noodles in a container of water in the fridge, to maintain crispness.

KOHLRABI

Kohlrabi contains more vitamin C than oranges and has good levels of the minerals copper, calcium, potassium, manganese, iron and phosphorus. It has a lovely earthy and refreshing taste and is great mixed through slaws, salads and your favourite pasta sauce or stir-fry.

Peel off the outer skin and slice a little bit off each end so it sits securely on the spiraliser. Kohlrabi has a firm flesh, so don't be afraid to use some pressure when spiralising. You can use all blades for this vegetable; however, it's best to use the thick noodle blade or the straight/ribbon blade if cooking the kohlrabi. Roast the noodles in a preheated 180°C oven for 5–6 minutes until cooked through. Alternatively, blanch them in simmering bone broth or salted water for 1 minute; or sauté them in a little quality oil or fat in a frying pan over medium heat until al dente, 1–2 minutes.

Raw spiralised kohlrabi lasts for 4–5 days stored in an airtight container or snap-lock bag in the fridge. To maintain their crisp texture, you can also store the noodles in a container filled with water in the fridge.

PARSNIP

Parsnips contain a wide variety of vitamins, minerals and nutrients – including dietary fibre, folate, potassium and vitamin C – and are good for heart health and weight loss.

They are great to spiralise as they perfectly complement a lot of the sauces and toppings in this book. The firm texture of parsnips makes them very easy to put through a spiraliser. Parsnip noodles are best eaten cooked and can be spiralised using any blade you wish to choose. I prefer the thick noodle blade as the parsnip looks like spaghetti when cooked and the kids can't tell the difference. Blanch the parsnip noodles in simmering bone broth or salted water for 30 seconds; alternatively, pan-fry them with a little coconut oil or fat until almost cooked through. Drizzle over a little extra-virgin olive oil to finish and they are ready to eat, plain or mixed through your favourite sauce or topping.

Store raw parsnip noodles in an airtight container or snap-lock bag in the fridge for 4–5 days.

PUMPKIN

Pumpkin is a rich source of minerals, like copper, calcium, potassium, phosphorus, and health-benefiting vitamins.

Pumpkin has a firm texture and is slightly trickier to spiralise than other vegetables used in this book. Use the thick noodle blade to spiralise pumpkin. Remove all the skin and seeds and trim the pumpkin into a slightly round 5 cm x 5 cm piece, which will make it easier to turn when spiralising. Don't discard the off-cuts as they can be used in other dishes, such as soups, sauces or mash. Pumpkin noodles are best eaten cooked. Pan-fry the noodles in a little quality oil or fat over medium heat until cooked through. You can also lightly drizzle olive oil over the noodles, then roast them in the oven preheated to 180°C for 5 minutes; alternatively, blanch them in simmering bone broth or salted water for 30–40 seconds until cooked through. Season with sea salt and freshly ground black pepper. Pumpkin noodles are lovely in salads, curries, soups and bakes.

Store raw pumpkin noodles in an airtight container or snap-lock bag in the fridge for 4–5 days.

RADISH

Radishes are a good source of vitamin C, which helps maintain cardiovascular health by controlling blood cholesterol levels. They are also rich in fibre, folate, potassium, magnesium, copper, manganese and calcium. Radishes aren't very large, but they are easy to spiralise and have a perfect, round shape that fits well on a spiraliser. Slice a little off each end to flatten evenly before spiralising. The thin and thick noodle blades and the straight/ribbon blade all work well. Radish noodles are perfect for salads and are best served raw.

Raw spiralised radish lasts for about 4–5 days stored in a container filled with water in the fridge, which helps to maintain their crisp texture.

SQUASH

Yellow squash are from the same family as pumpkin and zucchini and have a small, slightly flattened top and scalloped edges. Both skin and flesh are edible and have a similar flavour and texture to zucchini. Squash are an excellent source of vitamin C and contain dietary fibre.

Slice a little bit off each end of the squash so it can fit securely on the spiraliser. Enjoy squash raw or cooked and spiralise into thin or thick noodles or ribbons. If you prefer your squash cooked, blanch the noodles in simmering bone broth or salted water for 20–30 seconds; alternatively, sauté them in a frying pan along with your chosen sauce until al dente.

Store the prepared noodles in an airtight container or snap-lock bag for 4–5 days in the fridge.

SWEDE

Swedes are a beautiful root vegetable that belong to the cabbage family and have purple skin and firm white flesh. They are a great source of vitamins A and C, calcium, potassium and fibre.

It is super easy to spiralise swedes using any of the blades. You don't need to peel off the skin, I like leaving it on, just make sure it's well washed. Slice a little bit off the top and bottom before placing the swede on the spiraliser.

It's best to cook swede noodles, but they can be eaten raw and used in salads and slaws. Pan-fry the swede noodles in a little olive oil, tossing occasionally, until the noodles are al dente, about 1–2 minutes. You can also blanch the noodles in simmering bone broth or salted water for 30 seconds.

Raw spiralised swede noodles last for 4–5 days stored in an airtight container or snap-lock bag in the fridge. You can also store the noodles in a container filled with water in the fridge, as that will maintain their crisp texture.

SWEET POTATO

Sweet potatoes are large, starchy root vegetables that are packed with fibre, which helps to reduce high levels of cholesterol in the body. They are also packed full of vitamins such as A and C.

Sweet potato is best eaten cooked, either roasted or pan-fried. Peel the skin and use a thicker blade when spiralising. Preheat the oven to 180°C. Drizzle some coconut oil or quality fat over the noodles and toss well. Sprinkle on a little salt and roast in the oven for 5 minutes, or until cooked through. Alternatively, heat some quality oil or fat in a frying pan over medium–high heat. Add the noodles and toss occasionally for 6–8 minutes, or until cooked through. Season with salt.

Store raw sweet potato noodles in a snap-lock bag or airtight container in the fridge for 4–5 days.

TARO

Taro, the root of the taro plant, has a rough and woody skin and firm and starchy flesh with a beautiful nutty flavour. It is loaded with potassium, calcium, vitamins B, C and E, magnesium, manganese and copper.

Peel off the outer skin and spiralise the taro using the thick noodle blade or straight/ribbon blade. Taro must always be cooked, as it is toxic if eaten raw. Blanch in boiling bone broth or salted water for 2–3 minutes until cooked through. You can also roast it in the oven preheated to 180°C for 6–7 minutes.

Raw spiralised taro lasts for 4–5 days stored in an airtight container or snap-lock bag in the fridge. You can also store the noodles in a container filled with water in the fridge, which helps maintain their crisp texture.

TURNIP

Turnips are rich in vitamin C, which is believed to help the body scavenge harmful free radicals, prevent cancers and inflammation and boost immunity. Turnips are very similar to swedes in shape and texture. They can be spiralised to any thickness you wish and are best eaten cooked. Slice a little bit off the top and bottom before placing the turnip on the spiraliser; this will help the turnip sit nicely as it goes through the spiraliser.

Pan-fry the turnip noodles in a little quality oil over medium heat and cook, tossing occasionally, until the noodles are al dente, about 1–2 minutes. You can also blanch the noodles in simmering bone broth or salted water for 30 seconds.

Raw spiralised turnip lasts for 4–5 days stored in an airtight container or snap-lock bag in the fridge. To help maintain their crisp texture, you can also store the noodles in a container filled with water in the fridge.

ZUCCHINI

Zucchini are an outstanding source of antioxidants, magnesium, vitamins A, B and C, folate and potassium.

Zucchini are among my favourite vegetables to spiralise, as they are easy to prepare and go with pretty much any sauce or topping, such as bolognese, chicken and cashew stir-fry and pesto.

Before spiralising a zucchini, make sure you slice a little bit off each end, so it fits on the spiraliser. Enjoy zucchini raw or cooked and spiralise into thin or thick noodles or ribbons. If you prefer them cooked, blanch the noodles in simmering bone broth or salted water for 20–30 seconds; alternatively, sauté them in a pan with your chosen sauce until al dente. If you like them raw, a beautiful sun-dried tomato pesto or basil pesto mixed through the noodles is just sensational.

Store raw zucchini noodles in an airtight container or snap-lock bag in the refrigerator for 4–5 days.

Spiralising fruit with the kids can be a lot of fun – they love to see how many noodles one piece can produce. Here I use apple as the fruit accompaniment to a classic chia seed bircher. I like to use chia seeds instead of oats, as they are gentler on the digestive system and won't leave you feeling bloated. Apple oxidises and turns brown quickly, especially when there is so much surface area exposed. To prevent this, pop it into some acidulated water (filtered water with a squeeze of lemon juice).

COCONUT CHIA BOWL WITH APPLE & BERRIES

1 green apple, spiralised into thick noodles, plus extra to serve
3 tablespoons white or black chia seeds
1 tablespoon shredded coconut, plus extra to serve
125 g (½ cup) coconut yoghurt (for a recipe, see page 159), plus extra to serve
185 ml (¾ cup) almond milk

To serve
blueberries, raspberries and strawberries
almonds (activated if possible), chopped
pumpkin seeds and sunflower seeds (activated if possible)

You'll need to begin this recipe a day ahead.

Place the apple, chia seeds, coconut, coconut yoghurt and almond milk in a bowl and mix to combine. Cover with plastic wrap and refrigerate overnight.

The next morning, spoon the bircher into two bowls and top with some extra yoghurt and shredded coconut, along with the berries, extra apple spirals, almonds and seeds.

Serves 2

If there is one saving grace for busy, hungry families, it has to be the classic frittata. It is great for school or work lunches and perfect for when hungry teenagers ask what there is to eat, but the thing I love most is that you can put basically anything in it and it tastes brilliant. Last night's leftover roast beef, lamb or chicken? Tick! Things you need to use up in the fridge? Tick! Vegetables to get into the kids' diets? Tick! Give this frittata a whirl and make a big dish so you always have some on hand. Smother some homemade chilli sauce (see page 165) on top if you like it spicy.

FRITTATA WITH LOADS OF VEGGIES

1 carrot, spiralised into thin noodles
1 zucchini, spiralised into thick noodles
200 g kent or butternut pumpkin, spiralised into thick noodles
8 eggs
2 tablespoons chopped flat-leaf parsley leaves
80 ml coconut milk
sea salt and freshly ground black pepper
2 tablespoons coconut oil or good-quality animal fat*
1 large onion, sliced
2 garlic cloves, crushed
200 g rindless bacon or ham, chopped
1 large handful of baby spinach or kale leaves

* See Glossary

Preheat the oven to 200°C.

Combine the carrot, zucchini and pumpkin noodles in a bowl and set aside.

Crack the eggs into a bowl, add the parsley and coconut milk and whisk lightly. Season well with salt and pepper and set aside.

Melt the oil or fat in a large, ovenproof frying pan over medium heat. Add the onion and garlic and cook for 3–5 minutes until soft. Stir in the bacon or ham and cook for a further 3–5 minutes until lightly golden. Season with salt and pepper, add the noodles and spinach or kale and spread out evenly in the pan, then pour the egg mixture over the top. Transfer the pan to the oven and bake for 20 minutes, or until the frittata is puffed and golden and cooked through.

Leave the frittata to cool for at least 10 minutes, then cut into portions in the pan or turn out onto a chopping board, cut into portions and serve.

Serves 6

I eat sausages at least once a week. I just love 'em, as does everyone in my family. But we only eat sausages made the old-fashioned way – with pasture-raised meat, fat from pasture-raised animals, some spices and seasoning and maybe some onion and carrot. And that is it! No rice flour, no soy protein, no vegetable oils, no numbers, no preservatives, nothing fake.

SAUSAGES WITH CARAMELISED ONION & MUSTARD AIOLI

3 tablespoons coconut oil or good-quality animal fat*
8 paleo sausages of your choice
2 onions, sliced
sea salt and freshly ground black pepper
2 large handfuls of mixed salad leaves
1 small handful of baby bean sprouts, trimmed
3 radishes, spiralised into thin noodles
1 tablespoon apple cider vinegar
2 tablespoons extra-virgin olive oil
good-quality gherkins, julienned
sauerkraut (for a recipe, see page 164), to serve

Mustard aioli
120 g aioli (for a recipe, see page 157)
1 teaspoon wholegrain mustard or Fermented Mustard (page 160)

*See Glossary

Melt 1 tablespoon of coconut oil or fat in a large frying pan over medium heat and add the sausages. Cook for 10–12 minutes, turning occasionally, until golden brown and cooked through, then remove from the pan and keep warm, covered with foil.

Add the remaining coconut oil or fat and the onion to the pan and sauté, stirring occasionally, for 15 minutes, or until caramelised. Season with salt and pepper and set aside, covered with foil, in a warm spot.

To make the mustard aioli, mix the aioli and mustard in a bowl to combine.

To make the salad, place the salad leaves, sprouts and radish noodles in a bowl. Add the vinegar and olive oil and gently toss. Season with salt and pepper.

Arrange the salad on serving plates, place two sausages on each plate, dollop on some mustard aioli and serve with the caramelised onion, gherkins and sauerkraut.

Serves 4

This may look like a big breakfast but, in all honesty, it is just a wonderful, nutrient-dense meal that can be enjoyed at any time of day. I use sweet potato spirals to make these delicious rosti. Once you try them, they will become a firm family favourite that you can team with so many things, such as grilled fish and salad, to great effect.

THE PALEO BREAKFAST

2 tablespoons coconut oil or
   good-quality animal fat*
4 eggs
8 slices of bacon
2 garlic cloves, finely sliced
150 g baby spinach leaves
1 avocado, sliced into wedges
a few dill fronds
fermented vegetables of your
   choice (for recipes, see
   pages 58–63) (optional)

Sweet potato rosti
sea salt and freshly ground
   black pepper
600 g sweet potato, spiralised
   into thick noodles
2 eggs, at room temperature
2 tablespoons coconut oil or
   good-quality animal fat*

* See Glossary

To make the rosti, mix ½ teaspoon of salt through the sweet potato noodles and allow to stand for 10 minutes to draw out the liquid from the sweet potato. Squeeze out all the excess moisture from the sweet potato and place in a bowl. Add the eggs and some pepper and mix well. Melt half the oil or fat in a large, non-stick frying pan over medium–high heat. Spoon in 2 tablespoons of sweet potato mixture for each rosti and shape into eight patties. Cook, in batches of four, for 2 minutes until golden on the underside. Turn and cook for another 2 minutes until crisp and golden, then remove from the pan and keep warm.

Melt 1 tablespoon of oil or fat in the same pan over medium heat. Crack in the eggs and fry for 2–3 minutes, or until cooked to your liking. Season with salt and pepper.

Melt 2 teaspoons of the remaining oil or fat in another large, non-stick frying pan over medium–high heat. Add the bacon and fry for 3 minutes on each side until slightly coloured, cooking for longer if you like it crispy. Remove from the pan, drain on paper towel and keep warm. Melt the remaining oil or fat in the pan, add the garlic and cook until fragrant, about 20 seconds. Stir in the spinach and cook until it wilts, 1–2 minutes. Season with salt and pepper.

To serve, divide the spinach among warm serving plates, then top with two slices of bacon, two sweet potato rosti and a fried egg. Divide the avocado slices between the plates and sprinkle on some salt, pepper and dill. Serve with some fermented vegetables on the side, if desired.

Serves 4

Whenever I make a stir-fry, I love to use Chinese five spice. You can make your own using star anise, cloves, cinnamon (or cassia bark), Sichuan peppercorns and fennel seeds. If you want to get really fancy, then you can also add ginger, turmeric, licorice, cardamom and orange zest to make it Chinese ten spice. Cooking your mince with these spices will take the meal to another level entirely. And with the addition of vegetable noodles, fried eggs and some chilli sauce, I am sure this quick stir-fry will fast become a breakfast favourite.

STEAK & EGGS, MY WAY

3 tablespoons coconut oil or good-quality animal fat*, plus extra if needed
2 eggs
2 small red chillies, finely sliced, plus extra to serve
3 garlic cloves, finely chopped
400 g beef mince
125 ml (½ cup) chicken bone broth (for a recipe, see page 158)
1 teaspoon fish sauce, or to taste
1 teaspoon tamari or coconut aminos* (optional)
1 teaspoon honey (optional)
¼ teaspoon Chinese five spice
2 large handfuls of Thai basil leaves
1 large carrot, spiralised into thin noodles
2 Lebanese cucumbers, spiralised into thin noodles

To serve
1 handful of coriander leaves
sriracha chilli sauce (for a recipe, see page 165)
½ lime, cut into wedges

* See Glossary

Heat a wok or large frying pan over medium–high heat. Add 1 tablespoon of oil or fat and swirl it around the pan. Crack an egg into the centre and fry for 1–2 minutes, or until cooked to your liking, shaking the pan gently to prevent the egg from sticking. Carefully lift out the egg with a spatula and transfer to a plate to keep warm. Repeat with the remaining egg, adding a little more oil if needed.

Return the pan to high heat, add the remaining oil or fat and swirl it around the pan. Add the chilli and garlic and cook until fragrant, 1 minute. Mix in the beef and stir-fry for 2 minutes until brown, then pour in the broth and simmer for 3 minutes. Stir in the fish sauce, tamari or coconut aminos (if using), honey (if using) and Chinese five spice. Add the basil and carrot and cook for 30 seconds, or until the basil has wilted. Remove the pan from the heat and toss through the cucumber noodles.

Divide the beef stir-fry between serving plates and top each portion with a warm fried egg. Sprinkle on some extra chopped chilli and the coriander leaves. Serve with the sriracha sauce and lime wedges on the side.

Serves 2

Mushrooms and eggs are a wonderful way to start the day, as mushrooms are loaded with essential vitamins and minerals and eggs provide quality fat and protein. I've teamed these with parsnip spaghetti to turn this into a nourishing breakfast that will keep you going all day. Serve with a side of fermented veg, and if you want to add more protein, a minute steak or some snags make a welcome accompaniment.

MUSHROOMS, KALE & POACHED EGGS WITH SPAGHETTI

20 g dried porcini mushrooms
2 tablespoons apple cider vinegar
4 eggs
4 tablespoons coconut oil or good-quality animal fat*
300 g portobello mushrooms
1 onion, finely chopped
3 garlic cloves, finely chopped
1 teaspoon finely chopped thyme
100 g kale, stalks removed, leaves roughly chopped
125 ml (½ cup) chicken bone broth (for a recipe, see page 158)
sea salt and freshly ground black pepper
1 tablespoon olive oil
60 g pine nuts (activated if possible), toasted
2 tablespoons truffle oil
1 small handful of flat-leaf parsley leaves

Spaghetti
1 litre (4 cups) chicken bone broth (for a recipe, see page 158) or water
4–5 parsnips, spiralised into thin noodles

* See Glossary

Soak the porcini mushrooms in 125 ml of water for 15 minutes. Drain, reserving the soaking liquid.

Bring a large saucepan of salted water to the boil, pour in the vinegar and reduce the heat to medium–low so the water is just simmering. Crack an egg into a cup. Stir the simmering water in one direction to form a whirlpool and drop the egg into the centre. Repeat with the remaining eggs. Poach for 3 minutes, or until the eggs are cooked to your liking. Remove the eggs with a slotted spoon and drain on paper towel.

For the spaghetti, bring the broth or salted water to the boil in a saucepan, add the parsnip noodles and cook for 30 seconds. Drain, reserving the broth for another use, and keep the noodles warm until needed.

Melt 2 tablespoons of coconut oil or fat in a large frying pan over medium heat. Add the portobello mushrooms and fry, continuously tossing, for 2 minutes until golden. Remove the mushrooms from the pan and transfer to a plate.

Wipe the pan clean, add the remaining coconut oil or fat and melt over medium heat. Add the onion and sauté for 5 minutes until soft. Stir in the garlic, thyme and porcini and cook for 30 seconds until fragrant. Add the kale, broth and the reserved porcini soaking liquid and cook, stirring occasionally, for 3–4 minutes until the kale wilts. Return the portobello mushrooms to the pan and toss through. Season with a good amount of salt and pepper. Tip in the parsnip spaghetti, add the olive oil and toss to combine.

Divide the spaghetti between serving dishes and top each with a poached egg. Sprinkle on the pine nuts, drizzle on the truffle oil and scatter over some more pepper and the parsley.

Serves 4

SOUPS

For many years I have been saying that food is medicine for our bodies. Chicken soup, one of the world's most-loved dishes, is rich in so many nutrients that our bodies can only thrive when we include it in our diets. This combination of gut-strengthening chicken bone broth, an abundance of vegetables and a small amount of well-sourced meat and quality fat will have you laughing all the way to good health. Also try this recipe with fish or beef.

CHICKEN & VEGETABLE
NOODLE SOUP

2 tablespoons coconut oil or good-quality animal fat*
1 onion, finely chopped
3 garlic cloves, crushed
1 tablespoon finely grated ginger
1.75 litres (7 cups) chicken bone broth (for a recipe, see page 158), plus extra if needed
500 g shredded poached chicken
sea salt and freshly ground black pepper
2 large carrots, spiralised into thin noodles
2 zucchini, spiralised into thin noodles
300 g pumpkin, spiralised into thin noodles
2 parsnips, spiralised into thin noodles
1 handful of flat-leaf parsley leaves

* See Glossary

Melt the oil or fat in a large stockpot over medium heat. Add the onion, garlic and ginger and cook, stirring occasionally, for 6 minutes until the vegetables are soft but not browned. Pour in the broth and bring to the boil, then reduce the heat to low and simmer for 20 minutes.

Add the chicken to the pot and continue to simmer for another 2 minutes until the chicken is heated through. Season with salt and pepper.

Arrange the noodles in separate piles, place in the broth, cover with a lid and blanch for 30–60 seconds until just cooked through (the carrot and pumpkin will take a little longer to cook than the zucchini).

Transfer the noodles to serving bowls, ladle over the hot chicken broth and serve with the parsley and some freshly ground black pepper.

Serves 6–8

I think everyone has tried miso soup, but many people don't realise how simple this warm, delicious bowl of goodness is to make. A good homemade bone broth – made from chicken or fish bones – is paramount, as this is where the goodness and flavour come from. Make sure you use a top-quality, organic, fermented miso paste. Then it is just a matter of popping in some vegetables that you love and, of course, the essential seaweed, which gives miso soup its unique texture.

SPICY MISO SOUP

1 litre (4 cups) chicken or fish bone broth (for a recipe, see page 42 or 158)
3 teaspoons dried wakame*
6 fresh shiitake mushrooms, sliced
2 spring onions, finely sliced
1 tablespoon sriracha chilli sauce (for a recipe, see page 165)
125 g miso paste
½ daikon (about 350 g), spiralised into thick noodles

To serve
black sesame seeds, toasted
a few drops of sesame oil
chilli flakes (optional)

* See Glossary

Bring the broth to the boil in a large saucepan over medium heat. Add the wakame and simmer for 5 minutes until it has expanded. Mix in the shiitake mushrooms and spring onion and cook for 2–3 minutes until just tender. Stir in the sriracha, then add the miso – to distribute it evenly in the water, push it through a sieve into the pan. Cook, stirring, for about 1–2 minutes, or until the miso has dissolved.

Add the daikon noodles to the broth and cook for a further 30 seconds or until almost cooked through.

Divide the daikon noodles between warm bowls and pour over the soup. Scatter over some sesame seeds, add a dash of sesame oil and sprinkle on some chilli flakes (if using).

Serves 4

TIPS

If you're following a paleo lifestyle and would prefer not to use miso paste, simply replace it with some curry paste and a little coconut milk.

Play around with different ingredients based on what's in season and what you have in the fridge. Try this soup with seafood, such as cooked prawns. Bok choy is also a great addition, or enjoy it with some kimchi on the side.

Pho (pronounced as a quick 'fur'), the Vietnamese national breakfast, is a bone broth that is simmered for many hours to develop a deep, rich flavour. With the addition of freshly sliced meat and loads of vegetables, this beats a sugary bowl of cereal hands down.

VIETNAMESE PHO

2 kg beef bones, cut into 8 cm lengths (ask your butcher to do this)
2 pieces of cassia bark* or 2 cinnamon sticks
1 tablespoon coriander seeds
1 tablespoon fennel seeds
6 star anise
6 green cardamom pods
8 whole cloves
2 tablespoons coconut oil
6 x 120 g boneless beef short ribs
500 g oxtail, cut into 5 cm lengths (ask your butcher to do this)
2 onions, chopped
80 g ginger, finely sliced
3½ tablespoons fish sauce
2½ tablespoons coconut sugar
sea salt and freshly ground black pepper
1 kg bone marrow, cut into 3 cm medallions (ask your butcher to do this)
4–5 carrots, spiralised into thin noodles

To serve
200 g beef eye fillet or sirloin, finely sliced
100 g bean sprouts, trimmed
1 large handful each of mint, coriander, Thai basil and Vietnamese mint leaves
1 handful of snow pea sprouts
1 handful of sliced spring onion
sriracha chilli sauce (for a recipe, see page 165)
2 bird's eye chillies, sliced
lime wedges

* See Glossary

Preheat the oven to 200°C.

Place the beef bones in a large tin and roast for 30 minutes. Remove from the oven and set aside.

Place the spices in a piece of muslin, tie into a bundle with kitchen string and set aside.

Heat the coconut oil in a large stockpot over high heat, add the short ribs and oxtail in batches and seal on each side for 1½ minutes until golden brown, then remove from the pot.

Add the onion and ginger to the pot and cook for 5 minutes until they get a bit of colour. Pour in 5 litres of water, add the roasted beef bones, short ribs, oxtail and spice bag and simmer, frequently skimming any scum from the surface, over low heat for 3 hours until the short ribs are tender. Remove the short ribs from the broth, place in a bowl of cold water (this will prevent them from drying out and darkening as they cool) and refrigerate until needed.

Continue to simmer the broth, skimming occasionally, for 1½–2 hours until well flavoured. Add the fish sauce and coconut sugar. Allow to cool slightly, then strain into a large bowl and season to taste. Remove the meat from the oxtail and set aside.

When you are almost ready to serve, preheat the oven to 200°C. Place the bone marrow on a baking tray, season both sides with salt and pepper and roast in the oven for 12 minutes until cooked through.

Return the broth to the pot, add the short ribs and oxtail meat and bring to the boil. Simmer until the meat is heated through. Add the carrot noodles and cook for 30–40 seconds until just cooked.

Fill serving bowls with the carrot noodles and short ribs, then top with the hot broth, the raw beef, the sprouts, herbs, snow pea sprouts, spring onion, roasted bone marrow and sriracha. Serve with the chilli and lime wedges on the side.

Serves 6

We try to have soup at least once a week, and we vary it each and every time. One of my all-time favourites is Thai coconut curry soup with seafood. Now, you can make your own curry paste, which I encourage, or you can buy a good-quality one that contains no nasties (look for organic brands that don't have vegetable oils in them). Then really all you need is some quality bone broth and the rest is so, so easy.

THAI FISH SOUP

1 tablespoon coconut oil
2 tablespoons Thai green curry paste
3 garlic cloves, finely chopped
1 tablespoon lime juice
600 ml coconut cream
800 g fish fillets (such as snapper, cod, flathead or barramundi), cut into 3 cm cubes
3 carrots, spiralised into thick noodles
bean sprouts, trimmed, to serve
1 handful of Thai basil leaves, to serve

Fish bone broth

1 kg fish heads and carcasses (such as cod, snapper or barramundi)
2 teaspoons fish sauce, plus extra if needed
1 large onion, finely sliced
1 teaspoon black peppercorns, lightly crushed
3 kaffir lime leaves, torn

To make the fish bone broth, place the fish heads and carcasses in a large saucepan with 1.75 litres of water. Add the fish sauce, onion, peppercorns and lime leaves and bring to simmering point. Simmer for about 30 minutes, skimming occasionally.

Meanwhile, melt the coconut oil in another large saucepan over medium heat. Add the curry paste and garlic and sauté until fragrant, about 1 minute. Remove from the heat.

Strain the fish broth into the pan with the curry paste and garlic, stir well and adjust the seasoning with extra fish sauce, if needed. Stir in the lime juice, coconut cream and fish fillets and simmer over low heat for 4–5 minutes until the fish is just cooked through. Be careful not to boil, as the coconut cream might separate and the fish might overcook. Add the carrot noodles and cook for 1–2 minutes until just tender.

Divide the carrot noodles between serving bowls, ladle over the hot soup and fish and serve with the bean sprouts and Thai basil leaves.

Serves 4

Sometimes I just feel like a nice big bowl of vegetable soup to give my digestive system a bit of a break. This super-nourishing recipe, which is perfect in the cooler months, cooks pumpkin and zucchini in a delicious and healing ginger and chicken bone broth or vegetable stock. If you want to make this more filling, then try adding some seafood, leftover roast chicken or pork, a little bacon or a poached egg. And if you want to make it spicier, you could add some red curry paste and coconut cream.

SPICED PUMPKIN & GINGER SOUP

2 tablespoons coconut oil
1 kg kent pumpkin, diced
1 carrot, diced
1 large onion, finely chopped
4 garlic cloves, crushed
1.3 litres chicken bone broth (for a recipe, see page 158) or vegetable stock
1½ tablespoons finely grated ginger, plus extra as desired
2 teaspoons ground cumin
½ teaspoon chilli flakes (optional)
sea salt and freshly ground black pepper
4 zucchini (about 600 g in total), spiralised into thin noodles
a few coriander sprigs, to serve
pumpkin seeds (activated if possible), to serve

Melt the coconut oil in a large saucepan over medium heat. Add the pumpkin, carrot, onion and garlic and sauté, stirring occasionally, for 10 minutes until the onion is soft. Stir in the broth or stock, ginger, cumin and chilli flakes (if using). Reduce the heat to low, cover and simmer, stirring occasionally, for 40 minutes until the pumpkin is tender. Season with salt and pepper.

Divide the zucchini noodles between serving bowls, ladle in the hot soup and serve with the coriander, pumpkin seeds and some pepper scattered over the top.

Serves 4

On a hot day could there ever be a more elegantly simple and satisfying soup than gazpacho? This Spanish classic makes the most of tomatoes – bursting with flavour at their peak in summer – by blending them with vinegar, garlic, chilli, capsicum and cucumber. Here I have added cucumber noodles and crabmeat, though I find all seafood is tremendous with this chilled soup. Leftover roast chicken works a treat, too.

GAZPACHO WITH CRAB & CUCUMBER NOODLES

2–3 Lebanese cucumbers, spiralised into thin noodles
2 tablespoons lemon-infused extra-virgin olive oil
200 g picked fresh crabmeat
baby basil leaves, to serve

Gazpacho
1 kg tomatoes
1 Lebanese cucumber, halved
2 garlic cloves
1 bird's eye chilli, deseeded (leave in some seeds if you like it spicy)
1 red capsicum, halved and deseeded
1 celery stalk
½ red onion
1 small handful of basil leaves
2½ tablespoons extra-virgin olive oil, plus extra to serve
1 teaspoon ground cumin
1 teaspoon celery seeds
1½ tablespoons apple cider vinegar
juice of 1 lemon
2 teaspoons Worcestershire sauce (for a recipe, see page 165)
sea salt and freshly ground black pepper

To make the gazpacho, roughly chop the tomatoes, cucumber, garlic, chilli, capsicum, celery, onion and basil. Place in the bowl of a food processor or in a blender, add the olive oil, cumin and celery seeds and puree until smooth. Pass through a sieve for a refined soup or leave a bit chunky (whatever you prefer). Add the vinegar, lemon juice and Worcestershire sauce and season with salt and pepper. Refrigerate until ready to use.

Toss the cucumber noodles with half the lemon-infused oil and season with a touch of salt.

Mix the remaining lemon-infused oil with the crabmeat and season with salt.

Ladle the chilled gazpacho into serving bowls and top with the cucumber noodles and crabmeat, then garnish with the baby basil. Sprinkle some pepper over the top and finish with a light drizzle of extra-virgin olive oil.

Serves 3–4

I love this spin on the classic pork and prawn dumpling soup, and I am sure you will too. Here the usual dumpling wrappers have been replaced with lightly blanched cabbage leaves, which add more flavour and healthy goodness to this already beautiful and nourishing broth. You can use green cabbage but Chinese cabbage (wong bok) is also a great option, as the leaves are a little thinner and more pliable. Have a play around with different proteins for the filling – try crab, scallops or chicken mince.

PORK, PRAWN & CABBAGE DUMPLING SOUP

800 ml chicken bone broth (for a recipe, see page 158)
1½ teaspoons tamari, plus extra if needed
1 teaspoon sesame oil
1 teaspoon finely grated ginger
freshly ground black pepper
1 bunch of choy sum (about 300 g), trimmed and cut into 5 cm lengths
1 swede, spiralised into thin noodles

Dumplings
150 g pork mince
200 g raw prawn meat
1 spring onion, chopped
1½ teaspoons grated ginger
1 teaspoon tamari
1 teaspoon fish sauce
1 teaspoon sesame oil
1 tablespoon tapioca flour*
½ large green cabbage, leaves separated
1 eggwhite, whisked

* See Glossary

To make the dumplings, place the pork, prawn meat, spring onion, ginger, tamari, fish sauce, sesame oil and tapioca flour in the bowl of a food processor and pulse a few times to finely chop and combine. Tip into a bowl, cover with plastic wrap and transfer to the refrigerator until needed. Cut out sixteen 9 cm rounds from the cabbage leaves. Bring a saucepan of salted water to the boil and blanch the cabbage rounds for 2–4 minutes to soften. Drain and lay flat on paper towel to soak up any excess water. Lay a cabbage round on a work surface and put 1 tablespoon of the pork and prawn mixture in the centre. Brush the edge with the eggwhite, fold over the cabbage to enclose the filling and place the dumpling on a plate. Repeat with the remaining cabbage rounds and pork and prawn mixture.

Combine the broth, tamari, sesame oil and ginger in a saucepan and simmer for 10 minutes. Season with pepper and adjust with a little extra tamari, if needed.

Meanwhile, bring a large saucepan of water to the boil, then turn down the heat to low. Add the choy sum and simmer for 3 minutes until tender. Remove with a slotted spoon and set aside. Now add the dumplings to the simmering water and cook for 3 minutes until cooked through. Remove and place on a plate, keeping warm. Add the swede noodles and cook for 30–40 seconds until just cooked through.

Divide the swede noodles, choy sum and dumplings between bowls, then pour over the chicken broth and serve.

Serves 4

If I could get every Australian family to eat mussels once a week, I would be a happy man. The quality of South Australian, Victorian and Tasmanian mussels is second to none, and that in my book is a good enough reason to eat more of them. They can handle a lot of flavour and are delicious when simply steamed. In this lovely soup the mussels are the hero, while the addition of saffron and the subtle flavour of the blended mussel meat make the dish come alive.

MUSSEL BROTH WITH SAFFRON, CHILLI & CORIANDER

2 tablespoons coconut oil or good-quality animal fat*
1 onion, finely chopped
1 long red chilli, deseeded and finely chopped (leave in some seeds if you like it spicy)
4 garlic cloves, chopped
4 tomatoes, chopped
pinch of saffron threads
150 ml white wine
700 ml fish or chicken bone broth (for a recipe, see page 42 or 158)
1 kg black mussels, scrubbed and debearded
200 ml coconut cream
sea salt and freshly ground black pepper
1 swede, spiralised into thin noodles
1 handful of coriander leaves

* See Glossary

Melt the oil or fat in a large saucepan over medium heat. Add the onion and cook for 6–7 minutes until soft. Stir in the chilli and garlic and sauté for 1 minute, then add half the tomato, the saffron and wine. Bring to the boil and cook until reduced by half, about 3 minutes.

Pour the bone broth into the pan and bring to the boil. Add the mussels and cover with a lid. Cook until the mussels open, about 3–4 minutes. Remove all the mussels from the pan, discarding any unopened mussels. Add the coconut cream and the remaining tomato to the broth, bring to a simmer and take off the heat.

Remove the mussels from their shells. Blend half the mussels with a ladleful of the broth in a blender until smooth, then strain through a fine sieve. Whisk the mussel puree back into the broth in the pan and season with salt and pepper.

Divide the swede noodles and the remaining mussels between serving bowls, then pour over the hot broth. Set aside for 2 minutes to allow the swede to cook through before serving. Serve with the coriander and a sprinkle of pepper.

Serves 4

You have to love a soup that is tasty, satisfying and nourishing – and fits all that into one big bowl. This delicious recipe, which takes its inspiration from China, packs a real flavour punch with Sichuan pepper and chillies. I have added swede and turnip here, but you could easily replace these with cabbage, mushrooms, pumpkin, sweet potato or zucchini.

SICHUAN BEEF SOUP

600 g beef brisket, gravy
  beef, rump or chuck steak,
  cut into 2 cm cubes
3 tablespoons tamari
2 teaspoons apple cider
  vinegar
2 tablespoons coconut oil or
  good-quality animal fat*
3 garlic cloves, finely chopped
1 onion, chopped
2.5 cm piece of ginger,
  julienned
1 carrot, finely chopped
1 celery stalk, finely chopped
1–2 long red chillies,
  deseeded and finely sliced,
  plus extra to serve
2 spring onions, finely sliced
1.25 litres (5 cups) beef or
  chicken bone broth (for a
  recipe, see pages 157–8)
½ teaspoon ground allspice
1 teaspoon coarsely ground
  Sichuan peppercorns
1 large swede, cut into 1 cm
  cubes
2 large turnips, spiralised into
  thin noodles
sea salt and freshly ground
  black pepper
½ baby cos lettuce, leaves
  separated and torn, to serve
1 handful of coriander leaves,
  to serve

* See Glossary

Place the beef in a bowl, mix through the tamari and vinegar, cover and marinate in the refrigerator for 30 minutes.

Melt the oil or fat in a very large saucepan over medium–high heat. Add the garlic, onion, ginger, carrot, celery and chilli to the pan and cook until softened, about 5 minutes.

Add the meat and marinade and cook for a further 5 minutes. Reduce the heat to medium, stir in half the spring onion and cook for 2 minutes. Add the broth, allspice and Sichuan pepper and bring to the boil. Turn down the heat to low and simmer gently for 2 hours until the meat is almost tender (do not allow the soup to boil or the beef will become tough). Add the swede and continue to cook for 20 minutes until the beef and swede are completely tender. Add the turnip noodles and cook for 1 minute, or until cooked through. Season with salt and pepper.

Divide the turnip noodles between serving bowls, ladle the soup over the top and serve with the cos, coriander, a little extra chilli and the remaining spring onion.

Serves 4

Ramen bars are the newest happening thing in the culinary world, and I could not be more happy. Why, you may ask? Well, the main element of ramen is the nourishing broth, which is full of gut-healing properties. It is also packed full of vegetables and well-sourced meat and, of course, let's not forget the addition of seaweed and egg, which makes this dish a winner in my book.

JAPANESE PORK RAMEN SOUP

1.6 litres chicken bone broth (for a recipe, see page 158)
1 piece of dried kombu*, rinsed
3 tablespoons bonito flakes*
3 tablespoons tamari
½ teaspoon Chinese five spice
1 teaspoon coconut sugar
1 x 600 g boneless pork shoulder or pork belly, skin removed and cut in half
10 fresh shiitake mushrooms
4 cm piece of ginger, julienned
100 g enoki mushrooms, trimmed
½ daikon, spiralised into thick noodles
sea salt
3 tablespoons dried wakame*
4 hard-boiled eggs, halved
1 spring onion, white part only, finely chopped
shiso leaves*, to serve
shichimi togarashi*, to serve

See Glossary

Pour the broth into a large saucepan and bring to the boil. Reduce the heat to low, add the kombu, bonito flakes, tamari, Chinese five spice, coconut sugar and pork, cover and simmer for 2½– 3½ hours until the pork is tender. Remove the pork from the liquid, discard all the fat and shred the meat. Cover with foil and set aside in a warm spot.

Strain the broth into another large saucepan and discard the bonito and kombu. If the flavour of the stock is too intense, simply add a little water. Place the pan over medium heat and bring to a simmer. Add the shiitake mushrooms and ginger and simmer for 10 minutes, then add the enoki mushrooms and daikon noodles and cook for 2 minutes until the vegetables are cooked through. Season with salt.

Meanwhile, place the wakame in 500 ml of cold water and soak for 10 minutes. Drain and set aside until needed.

Divide the mushrooms, daikon and ginger between serving bowls. Arrange the shredded pork, wakame and egg on top, then ladle on the broth and serve with the spring onion, shiso leaves and a few pinches of shichimi togarashi.

Serves 4

Fermented or cultured veggies are dirt cheap to make when using vegetables in season – and the flavour combinations are limitless. These carrots work a treat with Moroccan and Middle Eastern cuisine, but you could easily substitute some curry leaves, cinnamon and cardamom for an Indian flavour, or some rosemary and garlic to make them Italian.

FERMENTED CARROT WITH GINGER & POMEGRANATE

6 large carrots, spiralised into thin noodles
1½ teaspoons sea salt
2 tablespoons finely chopped mint
2 tablespoons finely grated ginger
80 g (½ cup) pomegranate seeds
1 sachet vegetable starter culture (2–5 g depending on the brand, see note)
1 small cabbage leaf, washed

You will need a 1.5 litre preserving jar with an airlock lid for this recipe. Wash the jar, lid and all utensils thoroughly in very hot water or run them through a hot rinse cycle in the dishwasher.

Place the carrot noodles in a large glass or stainless steel bowl. Sprinkle over the salt, mint, ginger and pomegranate seeds. Mix well, cover with plastic wrap and set aside while you prepare the culture.

Dissolve the starter culture in filtered water according to the packet instructions (the amount of water will depend on the brand you use). Add to the carrot mixture and mix well.

Fill the prepared jar with the carrot mixture, pressing down well with a large spoon or potato masher to remove any air pockets and leaving 2 cm of room free at the top. The carrot should be completely submerged in the liquid, so add more water if necessary.

Take the clean cabbage leaf, fold it up and place it on top of the carrot mixture, then add a small glass weight (a shot glass is ideal) to keep everything submerged. Close the lid and wrap a tea towel around the side of the jar to block out the light.

Store the jar in a dark place with a temperature of 16–23°C for 10–14 days. (You can place the jar in an esky to maintain a more consistent temperature.) Different vegetables have different culturing times and the warmer it is, the shorter the amount of time needed. The longer you leave the jar, the higher the level of good bacteria present. It's up to you how long you leave it – some people prefer the tangier flavour that comes with extra fermenting time, while others prefer a milder flavour.

Chill before eating. Once opened, the fermented carrot will last for up to 2 months in the fridge when kept submerged in the liquid. If unopened, it will keep for up to 9 months in the fridge.

Makes 1 x 1.5 litre jar

NOTE

Vegetable starter culture is used to kick-start the fermentation process when culturing veggies and is available from health food stores or online.

I beg you to get your hands on a green papaya and give this a whirl! Serve it on the side of a simple grilled piece of fish or some Asian-spiced chicken wings and this will become a firm favourite. And perhaps make one batch without chilli for the kids to enjoy as well.

FERMENTED GREEN PAPAYA

2 green papaya (about 800 g each), spiralised into thin noodles
2½ teaspoons sea salt
2 long red chillies, deseeded and finely chopped
1 tablespoon finely grated ginger
2 tablespoons finely chopped coriander
1 small cabbage leaf, washed

You will need a 1.5 litre preserving jar with an airlock lid for this recipe. Wash the jar, lid and all utensils thoroughly in very hot water or run them through a hot rinse cycle in the dishwasher.

Place the papaya noodles in a large glass or stainless steel bowl. Sprinkle on the salt, chilli, ginger and coriander. Mix well and, with your hands, massage the papaya mixture for 5 minutes to release some liquid.

Fill the prepared jar with the papaya mixture, pressing down well with a large spoon or potato masher to remove any air pockets. Pour in all the liquid from the bowl, leaving 2 cm of room free at the top. The papaya should be completely submerged in the liquid, so add some filtered water to the jar if necessary.

Take the clean cabbage leaf, fold it up and place it on top of the papaya mixture, then add a small glass weight (a shot glass is ideal) to keep everything submerged. Close the lid and wrap a tea towel around the side of the jar to block out the light.

Store the jar in a dark place with a temperature of 16–23°C for 5–7 days. (You can place the jar in an esky to maintain a more consistent temperature.) Different fruits and vegetables have different culturing times and the warmer it is, the shorter the amount of time needed. The longer you leave the jar to ferment, the higher the level of good bacteria present. It's up to you how long you leave it – some people prefer the tangier flavour that comes with extra fermenting time, while others prefer a milder flavour.

Chill the fermented papaya before eating. Once the jar is opened, the papaya, submerged in the liquid, will last for up to 2 months in the fridge. If unopened, it will keep for up to 9 months in the fridge.

Makes 1 x 1.5 litre jar

If you are not including fermented vegetables in your diet, then I encourage you to do a little research into their health benefits. Cultured beetroot is a beautiful way to start off. Try having a tablespoon on the side with your meals or pop some on top of a burger patty.

FERMENTED BEETROOT

1 teaspoon whole black
  peppercorns
6 large beetroot, spiralised
  into thick noodles
zest of 1 lemon
1½ teaspoons sea salt
1 sachet vegetable starter
  culture (2–5 g depending on
  the brand, see note)
1 small cabbage leaf, washed

NOTE

Vegetable starter culture is used to kick-start the fermentation process when culturing veggies and is available from health food stores or online.

You will need a 1.5 litre preserving jar with an airlock lid for this recipe. Wash the jar and all utensils thoroughly in very hot water or run them through a hot rinse cycle in the dishwasher.

Put the peppercorns in a small piece of muslin, tie into a bundle and set aside.

Place the beetroot noodles and lemon zest in a large glass or stainless steel bowl. Sprinkle over the salt, mix well, cover with plastic wrap and set aside while you prepare the culture.

Dissolve the starter culture in filtered water according to the packet instructions (the amount of water will depend on the brand you use). Add to the beetroot mixture with the muslin bag containing the peppercorns and mix well.

Fill the prepared jar with the beetroot mixture, pressing down well with a large spoon or potato masher to remove any air pockets and leaving 2 cm of room free at the top. The beetroot should be completely submerged in the liquid, so add more water if necessary.

Take the clean cabbage leaf, fold it up and place it on top of the mixture, then add a small glass weight (a shot glass is ideal) to keep everything submerged. Close the lid and wrap a tea towel around the side of the jar to block out the light.

Store the jar in a dark place with a temperature of 16–23°C for 10–14 days. (You can place the jar in an esky to maintain a more consistent temperature.) Different vegetables have different culturing times and the warmer it is, the shorter the time needed. The longer you leave the beetroot in the jar to ferment, the higher the level of good bacteria present. It's up to you how long you leave it – some people prefer the tangier flavour that comes with extra fermenting time, while others prefer a milder flavour.

Chill before eating. Once opened, the beetroot will last for up to 2 months in the fridge when kept submerged in the liquid. If unopened, it will keep for up to 9 months in the fridge.

Makes 1 x 1.5 litre jar

Once you've made this salad you will never look at a cucumber in the same way again. It takes only a minute or so to make the dressing and another minute or two to spiralise the cucumber into noodles, yet when combined the taste is amazing. If you want to make this dish really special, a spoonful of salmon or trout roe is sensational, while some cured or smoked salmon or a can of sustainable tuna work a treat, too.

CUCUMBER NOODLES WITH SESAME DRESSING

4–5 Lebanese cucumbers, spiralised into thin noodles
1 large handful of mint leaves, torn
1 handful of baby spinach leaves
1 teaspoon white sesame seeds, toasted

Sesame dressing
3 tablespoons hulled tahini
2 tablespoons lemon juice
1 tablespoon olive oil
1 teaspoon tamari
1 garlic clove, very finely chopped
½ teaspoon honey, or to taste (optional)
sea salt and freshly ground black pepper

To make the sesame dressing, place the tahini, 3 tablespoons of water, the lemon juice, olive oil, tamari, garlic and honey (if using) in a bowl and mix until smooth. Season with salt and pepper.

Combine the cucumber noodles with the dressing, mint, spinach leaves and sesame seeds and gently toss.

Arrange the noodles on individual serving plates or a platter and serve immediately.

Serves 2–4 as a side dish

Coleslaw would have to be, without a doubt, one of my all-time favourite salads. It goes with just about everything. Serve it on the side of a grilled piece of fish or some crispy fried chicken, or pop it next to your barbecued lamb chops or snags. You can flavour the dressing with whatever spices or sauces you like. Try fermented Korean hot chilli sauce (gochujang), or go Japanese with wasabi. Or what about adding some Sichuan peppercorns and Chinese five spice, or preserved lemon and baharat for a Moroccan slaw, or curry leaves and curry powder for an Indian slant, or chimichurri to go South American … You get the picture!

COLESLAW

1 large beetroot, spiralised into thin noodles
2 carrots, spiralised into thin noodles
½ celeriac, spiralised into thin noodles
1 kohlrabi, spiralised into thin noodles
¼ red cabbage, finely shredded
1 large handful of mint leaves, shredded
1 handful of flat-leaf parsley leaves, roughly chopped
2 teaspoons finely grated lemon zest
sea salt and freshly ground black pepper

Dressing
juice of 2 lemons
3 tablespoons chopped chervil
250 g (1 cup) aioli (for a recipe, see page 157)

Place the noodles and cabbage in a large bowl and cover with cold water. Set aside while you make the dressing.

To make the dressing, combine the lemon juice, chervil and aioli in a bowl and mix well.

Drain the vegetables and dry well with paper towel. Dry the bowl and replace the vegetables.

When ready to serve, add the herbs, lemon zest and dressing to the vegetables and season with salt and pepper. Toss well and pile onto a platter.

Serves 4–6

Ratatouille, a classic French dish of vegetables in a slightly sharp and sweet dressing, works very well with roast lamb, grilled seafood and roast chicken. You can also pop it on the side of some fried eggs for breakfast as a lovely way to add vegetables to your morning meal. I have added some carrot noodles to my ratatouille. You could take it one step further and spiralise all the veggies so that you have a spiral ratatouille feast on your plate.

RATATOUILLE
WITH CARROT NOODLES

1 large eggplant, cut into 2.5 cm thick rounds, then sliced into 5 mm pieces
sea salt and freshly ground black pepper
4 tablespoons coconut oil, melted
2 zucchini, halved lengthways, then sliced into 5 mm pieces
1 red onion, finely chopped
1 red capsicum, cut into 2.5 cm thick strips, then sliced into 5 mm pieces
3 garlic cloves, finely chopped
3 tomatoes, chopped
3 tablespoons red wine vinegar or apple cider vinegar
1 teaspoon coconut sugar or honey
4 tablespoons olive oil
1 tablespoon finely chopped basil
1 litre (4 cups) bone broth (for a recipe, see pages 157–8) or salted water
4–5 carrots, spiralised into thick noodles
2 tablespoons extra-virgin olive oil
1 handful of chopped flat-leaf parsley leaves, to serve

Place the eggplant in a bowl, sprinkle on 1½ teaspoons of salt and mix well. Leave for 20 minutes (this draws out excess moisture and stops the eggplant from becoming bitter and watery). Rinse well and pat dry with paper towel.

Heat half the coconut oil in a large, non-stick frying pan over medium–low heat. Add the eggplant and zucchini and cook, stirring occasionally, for 8 minutes until tender. Add a little more coconut oil if needed. Remove from the pan and drain on paper towel.

Add the remaining coconut oil and the onion to the pan and sauté for 2 minutes until the onion is soft. Stir in the capsicum and cook for 5 minutes, then add the garlic and tomato and cook, stirring occasionally, for a further 5 minutes.

Return the eggplant and zucchini to the pan and simmer, stirring every now and then, for 5 minutes until they are cooked through. Season with salt and pepper. Remove from the heat, then stir in the vinegar, coconut sugar or honey, olive oil and basil and mix well.

Meanwhile, bring the broth or salted water to the boil in a saucepan. Add the carrot noodles and cook for 1–2 minutes until almost cooked through. Drain, reserving the broth for another use, and transfer the noodles to a bowl. Toss through the extra-virgin olive oil.

Place the noodles on a serving platter, top with the ratatouille, sprinkle over the parsley and serve.

Serves 4

Parsnips make for a wonderful side or salad. Here, parsnip noodles are combined with a moreish beetroot pesto and an aromatic and texturally delightful dukkah to give you one seriously addictive vegetable hit. When I create a dish like this, the protein I serve it with plays second fiddle. I like to team this salad with barbecued lamb chops, turmeric and cumin-spiced chicken wings, or a simple pan-fried piece of fish with a big wedge of lemon. Enjoy with some fermented veggies (see pages 58–63) on the side.

PARSNIP NOODLES WITH BEETROOT PESTO & DUKKAH

1 litre (4 cups) beef or chicken bone broth (for a recipe, see pages 157–8) or salted water
6 parsnips (about 700 g), spiralised into thin noodles
2 tablespoons olive oil
1 large handful of mixed mint and coriander leaves, plus extra to serve
80 g (½ cup) almonds (activated if possible), toasted and chopped
60 g pumpkin seeds (activated if possible), toasted
3 tablespoons dukkah (for a recipe, see page 159)

Beetroot pesto
3 beetroot (about 400 g), peeled and chopped
½ teaspoon ground cumin
3 garlic cloves
30 g (¼ cup) sunflower seeds (activated if possible)
1 large handful of basil leaves
3 tablespoons pine nuts (activated if possible), toasted
220 ml olive oil
120 ml apple cider vinegar
sea salt and freshly ground black pepper

To make the pesto, combine all the ingredients together in the bowl of a food processor and whiz to a fine paste. Taste and adjust the seasoning if necessary. If the pesto is too thick, stir in a little water until you reach the desired consistency.

Bring the broth or salted water to the boil in a saucepan. Add the parsnip noodles and cook for 30 seconds, or until almost tender. Drain, reserving the broth for another use. Toss the noodles with the olive oil and season with salt.

Combine the beetroot pesto, herbs, almonds and pumpkin seeds with the parsnip noodles and gently toss. Arrange on a platter and sprinkle over the dukkah and some extra herbs.

Serves 4

Often we think of vegetable dishes as sides, when really we should see them as stars. This delicious stir-fry, which is easily good enough to have as a main meal, shows just how exciting veggie dishes can be. Let's celebrate the wide variety of vegetables that are available to us and have a ball cooking with the seasons, cooking to a budget and, most importantly, cooking for health.

ASIAN MUSHROOM STIR-FRY

3 tablespoons coconut oil
4 garlic cloves, finely chopped
3 spring onions, finely chopped
1–2 long red chillies, deseeded and sliced (leave the seeds in if you like it spicy)
100 g wood ear fungus, torn into pieces (see note)
100 g shimeji mushrooms, trimmed and separated
150 g oyster mushrooms, sliced
150 g fresh shiitake mushrooms, sliced
2 bunches of baby bok choy (about 500 g in total), roughly chopped
4–5 zucchini (about 700 g in total), spiralised into thin noodles
100 g enoki mushrooms, trimmed and separated
1 tablespoon white sesame seeds, toasted, to serve

Sauce
1 tablespoon finely grated ginger
3 tablespoons tamari or coconut aminos*
4 tablespoons chicken or beef bone broth (for a recipe, see pages 157–8) or water
1 tablespoon apple cider vinegar
1½ teaspoons coconut sugar
½ teaspoon chilli flakes

* See Glossary

To make the sauce, combine all the ingredients in a bowl and mix well. Set aside until needed.

Melt the oil in a wok or large frying pan over medium–high heat. Add the garlic, spring onion and chilli and sauté for 1 minute. Splash in a tablespoon of water, then add the wood ear fungus, shimeji, oyster and shiitake mushrooms and bok choy and sauté for 2–3 minutes until tender. Pour in the sauce, bring to the boil and add the zucchini noodles. Toss and cook for 1 minute until the noodles are just cooked through.

Arrange the stir-fry on serving plates, top with the enoki mushrooms and sprinkle on the sesame seeds.

Serves 4

NOTE

Brown and ear-shaped, wood ear fungus is commonly used in Chinese cuisine and is available in Asian grocers.

There are some intoxicating flavour combinations that are hard to beat. One of my all-time faves is roasted pumpkin paired with crispy sage leaves. Here, I put these two mouth-watering ingredients together and team them with earthy parsnip or swede spaghetti, toasted pine nuts and greens for good measure. If you want to step this up to the next level, crabmeat, bacon, pancetta or prawns make great additions.

ROASTED PUMPKIN, SAGE & CAVOLO NERO WITH SPAGHETTI

700 g butternut pumpkin, cut into 2 cm cubes
4 tablespoons coconut oil or good-quality animal fat*, melted
sea salt and freshly ground black pepper
1½ onions, sliced
4 garlic cloves, finely chopped
1 bunch of cavolo nero (about 300 g), stalks removed and leaves roughly chopped
1 litre (4 cups) chicken bone broth (for a recipe, see page 158) or water
4–5 parsnips or 2 swedes (about 600 g), spiralised into thin noodles
50 g (⅓ cup) pine nuts (activated if possible), toasted
1–2 teaspoons chilli flakes, plus extra if desired
3–4 tablespoons extra-virgin olive oil
juice of 1 lemon
16 Crispy Sage Leaves (page 143), to serve
Paleo Cheese (page 162), grated, to serve

* See Glossary

Preheat the oven to 180°C.

Place the pumpkin and 2 tablespoons of coconut oil or fat in a bowl and mix to coat evenly. Transfer the pumpkin to a baking tray in a single layer and season with salt and pepper. Bake in the oven for 12–15 minutes until tender. Remove from the oven and set aside until needed.

Heat the remaining coconut oil or fat in a large frying pan over medium–low heat. Add the onion and cook, stirring occasionally, for 10–12 minutes until caramelised. Stir in the garlic and sauté for 1 minute until fragrant, then add the cavolo nero and 3 tablespoons of water and continue to sauté for 2 minutes until the cavolo nero is just starting to wilt. Add the pumpkin, give the pan a good toss, then remove from the heat. Season with salt and pepper.

Meanwhile, bring the broth or salted water to the boil in a saucepan. Add the parsnip or swede spaghetti and cook for 1 minute, or until just cooked through. Drain, reserving the broth for another use, then gently toss the spaghetti with the sautéed vegetables. Add the pine nuts, chilli flakes, olive oil and lemon juice and toss again.

Divide the spaghetti between serving plates, sprinkle on the crispy sage leaves and add some paleo cheese to finish.

Serves 4

When I can get my hands on some awesome basil, the first thing I make is a dairy-free pesto – and heaps of it. (You can freeze it in ice-cube trays, if you like, for later use.) Pesto is a wonderful flavour bomb with so many uses. Toss it through roasted veggies or a salad, or have it on the side of a sensational grilled fish fillet or lamb chop. You simply cannot beat it. Here I have teamed the pesto with beetroot spirals and sautéed kale to create a delicious salad that will surely make you, your friends and your family feel wonderful.

ROASTED BEETROOT SALAD
WITH **PESTO**

3 large beetroot (about 600 g), spiralised into thick noodles
4 tablespoons coconut oil, melted
sea salt and freshly ground black pepper
1 bunch of kale (about 300 g), stalks removed and leaves torn
2 garlic cloves, finely chopped
50 g (1/3 cup) pine nuts (activated if possible), toasted
1 handful of mint leaves

Pesto
2 garlic cloves, chopped
1 large handful of basil leaves
1 large handful of mint leaves
1/2 teaspoon ground cumin
60 g pine nuts (activated if possible), toasted
120 ml olive oil
1 1/2 tablespoons lemon juice
1–2 pinches of chilli flakes

Preheat the oven to 180°C.

To make the pesto, combine all the ingredients in the bowl of a food processor and whiz to make a thick, fragrant paste.

Place the beetroot spirals in a bowl, add 2 tablespoons of coconut oil and toss through until evenly coated. Transfer the beetroot to a baking tray, spread out evenly in a single layer, then roast in the oven for 8–10 minutes, or until just cooked through. Season with salt and pepper.

Meanwhile, melt the remaining coconut oil in a large, non-stick frying pan over medium heat. Add the kale and sauté for 2 minutes until slightly wilted, then stir in the garlic and sauté for a further 30 seconds. Season with salt and pepper.

Combine the beetroot spirals, kale, pine nuts and half the pesto in a bowl and gently mix. Place on a large platter, drizzle over more pesto and scatter on the mint leaves. Leftover pesto can be frozen or stored in a jar in the fridge for up to 3 days.

Serves 4 as a side

Caponata was one of the first vegetable dishes I learned to make at culinary college. I can still remember my first mouthful – it was sweet, sour and salty with the most amazing mouth feel, and it made me an instant eggplant and zucchini fan. If you are looking at ways to get the kids to appreciate vegetable dishes, then give this one a go. Serve alongside some roast lamb, snags or a simple roast chicken.

CAPONATA WITH ZUCCHINI NOODLES

2 large eggplants, cut into 2 cm cubes
sea salt and freshly ground black pepper
280 ml coconut oil, melted
1 onion, diced
1 celery stalk, diced
3 garlic cloves, finely chopped
1 red capsicum, diced
4 roma tomatoes, diced
1 x 400 g can whole peeled tomatoes, chopped
80 g (½ cup) pitted kalamata olives, halved
1 tablespoon honey
4 zucchini (about 600 g in total), spiralised into thick noodles
2 tablespoons currants
1 handful of mixed flat-leaf parsley and basil leaves, chopped, plus extra to serve
2 tablespoons salted baby capers, rinsed and patted dry
3 tablespoons pine nuts (activated if possible), toasted
3 tablespoons red wine vinegar
3 tablespoons extra-virgin olive oil

Place the eggplant in a bowl, mix in 1 teaspoon of salt and allow to stand for 15 minutes.

Heat 250 ml of coconut oil in a large frying pan over medium–high heat, add the eggplant in batches and shallow fry, stirring occasionally, until golden, 6–7 minutes. Remove from the pan with a slotted spoon and drain on paper towel.

Heat the remaining coconut oil in another large frying pan over medium heat. Add the onion and celery and fry for 5 minutes until lightly golden. Add the garlic and cook until fragrant, then reduce the heat to low and stir in the capsicum, diced tomato, canned tomatoes, 250 ml of water, the olives and honey and cook for 15 minutes until the vegetables are soft. Stir in the zucchini noodles and cook for 1 minute until they are just cooked through.

Remove the pan from the heat and gently mix in the eggplant, currants, herbs, capers, pine nuts, vinegar and olive oil. Season with salt and pepper and scatter over some extra herbs, if desired.

Serves 4

Now, we are getting a little fancy with this recipe. By adding in some smoky notes with the paprika and other spices, the humble carrot becomes the star. I recommend serving this alongside a roast pork shoulder or pork belly spiced with cumin or fennel seeds, a whole roasted fish, or tossed with some squid and prawns that have been cooked on the barbecue.

ROASTED CARROT WITH SMOKY ALMOND DRESSING

2 carrots (about 300 g), spiralised into thick noodles
2 purple carrots (about 300 g), spiralised into thick noodles
140 ml coconut oil or good-quality animal fat*
sea salt and freshly ground black pepper
3 French shallots, finely chopped
6 garlic cloves, finely chopped
1 spring onion, finely chopped
1 tablespoon finely grated ginger
1 teaspoon chilli flakes
1 teaspoon smoked paprika
¼ teaspoon ground turmeric
70 g almonds (activated if possible), chopped
1½ tablespoons apple cider vinegar

* See Glossary

Preheat the oven to 180°C.

Place the carrot noodles in a bowl, toss through 1 tablespoon of oil or fat and season with salt and pepper. Transfer the noodles to a baking tray and bake in the oven for 6–8 minutes, or until almost cooked through.

Meanwhile, melt the remaining oil or fat in a frying pan over medium heat. Add the shallot and sauté for 5 minutes until translucent. Stir in the garlic, spring onion and ginger and continue to sauté for 30 seconds until the vegetables are soft. Next add the chilli flakes, smoked paprika, turmeric and almonds and cook for 30 seconds until fragrant. Remove from the heat and mix in the vinegar. Season with salt and pepper.

Pour the smoky almond dressing over the carrot noodles, toss through and serve.

Serves 4 as a side

Fish and salad. Has there ever been a healthier combination of ingredients that tastes so awesome? Here I have rolled some spankin' fresh tuna in an umami bomb of toasted nori seaweed and combined it with the usual suspects – cucumber, avocado, chilli and fresh herbs. The dressing brings it all together and takes only a minute or two to make.

TUNA SASHIMI WITH CUCUMBER SALAD & BONITO

1 nori sheet*
500 g sashimi-grade tuna, sliced into 3 long pieces

Yuzu dressing
3 tablespoons yuzu juice* (see tip)
3 tablespoons tamari
3 tablespoons extra-virgin olive oil
2 teaspoons sesame oil
1 tablespoon finely grated ginger
a good pinch of freshly ground white pepper

Cucumber salad
2 Lebanese cucumbers, spiralised into thin noodles
1 avocado, cut into 1 cm dice
1 green jalapeno chilli, deseeded and finely chopped
1 teaspoon white sesame seeds, toasted

To serve
2 tablespoons bonito flakes*
2 tablespoons salmon roe
shiso leaves* (optional)
freshly ground black pepper

* See Glossary

Cut the nori into three 7 cm x 20 cm strips. Lay the nori strips shiny-side down and short side towards you and place a piece of tuna lengthways in the centre. Wrap the nori over the tuna to enclose. Set aside.

To make the dressing, combine the ingredients in a jar, cover and shake well.

To make the salad, combine the cucumber noodles, avocado, jalapeno and sesame seeds in a bowl and gently mix in half the dressing. Set aside until needed.

Finely slice the nori-wrapped tuna and arrange on serving plates. Scatter on the bonito, pour the dressing over the tuna and serve with the salmon roe, shiso leaves (if using), a little black pepper and the cucumber salad on the side.

Serves 4

TIP

Yuzu juice is available from Asian grocers. If you can't get your hands on some, simply substitute the same quantity of lemon, lime, grapefruit or orange juice, or the juice of any other citrus fruit.

If you are searching for something quick and easy to prepare when guests pop over, then look no further than this refreshing little salad, which can be on the table in a matter of minutes. The combination of lemon, capers, fresh herbs, chilli, fennel and cucumber makes for the perfect backdrop to the lightly charred squid (or whatever other seafood you may choose). Give it a whirl next time you have guests and the weather is warm.

SQUID SALAD WITH CUCUMBER, FENNEL & CAPERS

600 g baby squid, cleaned and tubes sliced into strips
sea salt and freshly ground black pepper
3 Lebanese cucumbers, spiralised into thin noodles
1 large fennel bulb, finely sliced
7 semi-dried tomatoes, marinated in olive oil, finely sliced
½ red onion, finely sliced
2 long red chillies, deseeded and finely chopped
3 tablespoons salted baby capers, rinsed and patted dry
1 handful of dill fronds
1 handful of flat-leaf parsley leaves
2 large handfuls of mixed salad leaves
1 preserved lemon quarter, flesh removed and rind finely sliced
4 tablespoons lemon-infused extra-virgin olive oil
3 tablespoons apple cider vinegar

Marinade
2 tablespoons coconut oil, melted
2 long red chillies, deseeded and finely chopped
4 garlic cloves, finely chopped
zest and juice of 1 lemon

Season the squid with salt and pepper and place in a bowl. Add all the marinade ingredients to the bowl and toss to combine. Cover and transfer to the fridge to marinate for 30 minutes.

To make the salad, toss the cucumber noodles, fennel, semi-dried tomatoes, onion, chillies, capers, herbs, salad leaves and preserved lemon rind in a bowl. Add the lemon-infused olive oil and vinegar, season with salt and pepper and toss gently.

Place a frying pan over high heat and sauté the squid, in batches, for 2–3 minutes until cooked through and lightly charred. Add the lemon juice to the pan and toss with the last batch of squid. Tip into the salad, toss gently and serve immediately.

Serves 4

When the weather starts to heat up and you want to pop something that is refreshing, satisfying and utterly delicious on the table, then look no further than this simple Thai-inspired smoked trout salad. I encourage you to taste the dressing as you go so that you get to understand the balancing act of making a Thai-style dressing, with its notes of saltiness, sourness, heat and a little sweetness. You can replace the smoked trout with roast chicken or barbecued prawns, while if daikon is tricky to find, just substitute carrot instead.

SMOKED TROUT SALAD

1 hot-smoked rainbow trout, bones and skin removed, flesh flaked (about 250 g)
2 red Asian shallots, finely sliced
2 long red chillies, deseeded and julienned
1 large handful of mint leaves, torn
1 handful of Vietnamese mint leaves, torn
3 kaffir lime leaves, finely sliced
1 large handful of coriander leaves
½ daikon, spiralised into thin noodles
100 ml Nam Jim Dressing (page 161), plus extra if needed
4 tablespoons Crispy Shallots (page 159)
50 g trout roe or salmon roe

Combine the trout, shallot, chilli, mint, Vietnamese mint, kaffir lime leaves, coriander and daikon noodles in a bowl.

Dress the trout salad with the nam jim dressing, gently toss to combine, then place the salad in serving bowls and top with the crispy shallots and roe.

Serves 2–4

Surf and turf has never tasted so good. This Spanish number combines pork and prawns, and, while it may seem a little unusual, this pairing is used in many different cultures around the world – Chinese, Vietnamese and Portuguese being just a few examples. Here, to make this a memorable dish for the whole family, I have added a delicious sauce and some zucchini pappardelle to soak up all that flavour.

PRAWN & CHORIZO WITH SAFFRON SAUCE & PAPPARDELLE

300 ml chicken bone broth
  (for a recipe, see page 158)
2 pinches of saffron threads
2 tablespoons coconut oil or
  good-quality animal fat*
12 raw king prawns, shelled,
  deveined and halved
150 g chorizo sausage, cut
  into 1 cm cubes
1 red capsicum, diced
1 roma tomato, diced
1 large onion, chopped
4 garlic cloves, finely chopped
1 tablespoon tomato paste
1 teaspoon sweet paprika
1 tablespoon smoked paprika,
  plus extra to serve
1 small handful of flat-leaf
  parsley, stalks and leaves
  chopped separately
200 g cherry tomatoes, halved
sea salt and freshly ground
  black pepper
extra-virgin olive oil, for
  drizzling
½ lemon, cut into wedges

Zucchini pappardelle
1 litre (4 cups) chicken bone
  broth (for a recipe, see
  page 158) or salted water
4–5 zucchini (about 700 g in
  total), spiralised into ribbons

* See Glossary

Bring the broth to a simmer in a saucepan over medium heat. Remove from the heat, stir in the saffron and set aside to infuse for 5–10 minutes.

Melt 1 tablespoon of coconut oil or fat in a large frying pan over high heat, add the prawns and fry for 30 seconds on each side until slightly golden but still raw in the middle, then remove from the pan.

Wipe the pan clean and melt the remaining coconut oil or fat over medium–high heat. Add the chorizo and fry until golden and crispy, about 5 minutes. Stir in the capsicum, tomato, onion, garlic, tomato paste and sweet and smoked paprika and cook until the vegetables are soft, 2–3 minutes. Pour in the warm saffron-infused broth, add the chopped parsley stalks and bring to the boil. Add the cherry tomatoes and cook for 2 minutes, then return the prawns and cook for 1 minute more until the prawns are just cooked through and the cherry tomatoes have softened. Season with salt and pepper.

Meanwhile, to make the zucchini pappardelle, bring the broth or salted water to the boil in a saucepan. Add the zucchini ribbons and blanch for 10–20 seconds. Drain, reserving the broth for another use.

Arrange the zucchini pappardelle on serving plates, then top with the sauce. Scatter on the parsley leaves and serve with a drizzle of olive oil, a squeeze of lemon juice and a sprinkle of extra smoked paprika.

Serves 4

If you ever visit Hawaii, you must try the locals' favourite dish of poke (pronounced 'pokey'), which is a cross between a Tahitian marinated fish salad and a Japanese sashimi plate. The freshness of the produce makes this dish shine. Any fish is perfect, as long as you love eating it raw. Some of my favourites are tuna, kingfish, mackerel, cobia, flathead, snapper, whiting, coral trout, red emperor and alfonsino. You could also try squid, prawns, scampi or, my all-time favourite, sea urchin. To make this more substantial, add some chilled cauliflower rice or kelp noodles.

SALMON POKE

300 g sashimi-grade salmon, cut into small dice
½ avocado, cut into small dice
1 tablespoon sesame oil
2 teaspoons finely grated ginger
2 tablespoons yuzu juice*
2 tablespoons tamari or coconut aminos*
½ teaspoon chilli oil (for a recipe, see page 159) (optional)
2 tablespoons lemon-infused extra-virgin olive oil
3 Lebanese cucumbers, spiralised into thin noodles
1 teaspoon white and black sesame seeds, toasted
2 tablespoons salmon roe, to serve
coriander leaves, to serve

Wasabi aioli
70 g aioli (for a recipe, see page 157)
½ teaspoon wasabi

* See Glossary

To make the wasabi aioli, mix the ingredients in a small bowl.

Place the salmon in a chilled bowl. Add the avocado, sesame oil, ginger, yuzu juice, tamari or coconut aminos, chilli oil (if using) and lemon-infused olive oil. Mix well until combined.

Divide the cucumber noodles between small serving bowls. Top each portion with the salmon mixture, then spoon over any leftover dressing from the bowl. Add a dollop of wasabi aioli and serve with the sesame seeds, salmon roe and a few coriander leaves.

Serves 4

What I love most about this dish is the wonderful flavour of the sauce – the aromatic base of garlic, shallot, chilli, coriander and fish sauce that is finished with crabmeat, lime juice, lots of black pepper and yet more coriander. You can replace the crab with prawn meat if you like, or even chicken works a treat.

CRAB, CHILLI & CORIANDER SPAGHETTI

2 tablespoons coconut oil or good-quality animal fat*
4 garlic cloves, sliced
3 French shallots, sliced
1 long red chilli, deseeded and finely sliced
1 large handful of coriander, roots, stalks and leaves chopped separately
2½ tablespoons fish sauce
500 ml (2 cups) fish bone broth (for a recipe, see page 42)
15 cherry tomatoes, halved
2 swedes or 4 parsnips, spiralised into thin noodles
200 g picked fresh crabmeat
a splash of extra-virgin olive oil
4 coriander sprigs, to serve
lime halves, to serve
freshly ground black pepper

* See Glossary

Melt the coconut oil or fat in a large frying pan over medium–high heat and sauté the garlic, shallot, chilli and coriander root for 3 minutes until golden. Pour in the fish sauce and cook for 30 seconds to release the flavour. Add the broth and tomatoes, bring to the boil and cook for 5 minutes until the sauce is reduced and thickened.

Add the swede or parsnip spaghetti to the sauce and cook for 2–3 minutes until just tender. Stir in the crabmeat, olive oil and the rest of the chopped coriander and serve with the coriander sprigs, a squeeze of lime juice and a sprinkle of black pepper.

Serves 2

This is one of my favourite recipes in the whole book. It takes less than 15 minutes to pop on the table and it's a culinary triumph. This taste sensation combines dairy-free pesto with just-cooked zucchini spaghetti, plump and juicy prawns, and crunchy pistachios. You just have to try it to understand how seriously good it is.

SPAGHETTI WITH PRAWNS, PESTO & PISTACHIOS

4 tablespoons coconut oil
700 g raw king prawns, shelled and deveined, with tails intact
4–5 zucchini (about 700 g in total), spiralised into thin noodles

Pesto
2 garlic cloves, chopped
1 large handful of basil leaves, plus extra to serve
1 large handful of mint leaves
60 g pine nuts (activated if possible), toasted
120 ml olive oil
1½ tablespoons lemon juice
sea salt and freshly ground black pepper

To serve
extra-virgin olive oil
80 g (½ cup) pistachio nuts (activated if possible), toasted and roughly chopped
lemon wedges
chilli flakes (optional)

To make the pesto, place all the ingredients in the bowl of a food processor and whiz until the herbs and nuts are finely chopped. Taste and season with salt and pepper.

Melt 2 tablespoons of coconut oil in a large frying pan over medium–high heat. Season the prawns with salt and pepper, then cook, in batches, for 1 minute on each side until just cooked through. Remove the prawns from the pan and set aside, covered with foil to keep warm.

Wipe the pan clean and place over medium heat. Add the remaining coconut oil and the zucchini spaghetti and sauté for 2 minutes until the zucchini is almost cooked through. Season with a little salt and pepper. Remove from the heat, add the cooked prawns and the pesto and toss to combine.

Transfer the spaghetti mixture to a large platter or serving plates, drizzle on some extra-virgin olive oil, sprinkle over the pistachios, add a squeeze of lemon juice and scatter on some basil leaves and a few chilli flakes, if desired.

Serves 4

When I look at this dish, it screams 'Eat me! I'm healthy'. Fresh herbs and salad leaves, a homemade mustard dressing and good-quality protein in the form of tuna make this a wonderful salad to put together on a warm summer's day for lunch or dinner. If you want to bulk it out a little then feel free to add soft- or hard-boiled eggs along with some avocado for extra good fats.

TUNA SALAD

3 Lebanese cucumbers, spiralised into thin noodles

1 x 425 g can tuna in brine or olive oil, drained

2 large handfuls of mixed salad leaves

150 g semi-dried tomatoes in olive oil, drained

4 tablespoons salted baby capers, rinsed well and patted dry

½ red onion, finely sliced

1 handful of dill fronds

1 handful of basil leaves

freshly ground black pepper

1 lemon, cut into wedges, to serve

Mustard dressing

1 egg

1 egg yolk

2 tablespoons lemon juice

1 tablespoon apple cider vinegar

2 teaspoons Dijon mustard or Fermented Mustard (page 160)

sea salt

150 ml olive or macadamia oil

To make the dressing, place the egg, egg yolk, lemon juice, vinegar, mustard and a pinch of salt in a bowl and whisk to combine. Slowly drizzle in the oil and continue to whisk until the mixture begins to emulsify. Keep whisking and adding the oil slowly and consistently in a thin stream until the mixture is thick and looks like mayonnaise. (Alternatively, make this using a hand-held blender.) Set aside until needed.

Combine the cucumber, tuna, salad leaves, semi-dried tomatoes, capers, red onion and herbs in a bowl, pour on half the dressing and gently mix. Season with salt and pepper to taste.

Arrange the tuna salad on a large platter, drizzle on a little more dressing if needed and serve with some lemon wedges on the side.

Serves 4

TIP

Any remaining dressing can be stored in a jar in the refrigerator for up to 5 days.

These delicious Singapore noodles are made from zucchini noodles that are coated in the most amazing sauce. This is a wonderfully exciting textural dish, where all the components that work so well together vie for attention on your tastebuds.

SINGAPORE NOODLES

3 tablespoons coconut oil
2 eggs, lightly beaten
4 chicken thigh fillets, sliced
2 red Asian shallots, finely sliced
1 red capsicum, finely sliced
5 cm piece of ginger, finely grated
1–2 long red chillies, deseeded and finely chopped
3 garlic cloves, chopped
300 g raw king prawns, shelled and deveined
350 g Chinese broccoli (gai larn), roughly chopped
2½ tablespoons curry powder
1½ tablespoons tamari
1 teaspoon sesame oil
1 handful of bean sprouts, trimmed
4–5 zucchini (about 700 g in total), spiralised into thin noodles
sea salt and freshly ground black pepper
1 spring onion, finely sliced
1 handful of coriander leaves
lime wedges, to serve
sauerkraut (for a recipe, see page 164), to serve (optional)

Melt 1 tablespoon of coconut oil in a large frying pan or wok over medium–high heat. Pour in the egg and tilt the pan so the egg covers the base. Cook for a few minutes until the egg is set, then remove from the pan, slice into thin strips and set aside.

Increase the heat to high, add the remaining coconut oil and the chicken to the pan and stir-fry for 2 minutes, then stir in the shallot, capsicum, ginger, chilli and garlic and stir-fry for 3 minutes until the vegetables are soft.

Add the prawns and Chinese broccoli to the pan and stir-fry for 1 minute until the prawns just start to change colour. Stir in the curry powder, tamari and sesame oil and cook for 1 minute until the prawns are almost cooked through. Return the egg to the pan, add the bean sprouts, zucchini noodles and some salt and pepper and cook, tossing the pan occasionally, for 2 minutes until everything is heated through and well combined.

Arrange the Singapore noodles on a platter or on serving plates and sprinkle on the spring onion and coriander leaves. Serve with some lime wedges and sauerkraut on the side, if desired.

Serves 4

Vongole, or clams, are the unsung heroes of the seafood world.
One of the best and most-loved ways to eat them is in a simple Italian preparation,
like the one I share here. I have teamed the vongole with parsnip spaghetti,
which adds nutrition and earthiness to these amazing sea offerings.

SPAGHETTI VONGOLE

1 litre (4 cups) fish bone broth
(for a recipe, see page 42)
or salted water
5 parsnips (about 500 g),
spiralised into thin noodles
3 tablespoons olive oil
sea salt
3 tablespoons coconut oil or
good-quality animal fat*
4 garlic cloves, finely chopped
2 long red chillies, deseeded
and finely chopped
4 salted anchovy fillets,
rinsed, patted dry and finely
chopped
finely grated zest of 1 lemon,
plus extra to serve
4 tablespoons finely chopped
flat-leaf parsley leaves
800 g vongole (clams),
scrubbed
4 tablespoons white wine

* See Glossary

Bring the broth or salted water to the boil in a saucepan. Add the parsnip spaghetti and cook for 30 seconds until almost tender. Drain, reserving the broth for another use. Toss the spaghetti with a splash of olive oil and season with salt. Set aside.

Melt the coconut oil or fat in a large saucepan over medium–high heat, add the garlic and cook for 30 seconds until the garlic just starts to turn golden. Stir in the chilli, anchovy, lemon zest and parsley and cook for 10 seconds. Add the vongole, cook for about 30 seconds, then pour in the wine and cook, covered, for 1–2 minutes until all the vongole open (discard any that don't open). Remove the vongole from the pan and set aside in a bowl, covered with foil to keep warm. Simmer the sauce in the pan, stirring occasionally, over medium–high heat for 5 minutes until reduced by half.

Add the spaghetti to the sauce and cook, tossing the pan to coat the spaghetti in the sauce, for 1 minute until the spaghetti is heated through. Add the remaining olive oil and the vongole and toss well.

Serve on plates or a large platter and grate a little extra lemon zest over the top.

Serves 2

Most people love pasta but, when you think about it, nutritionally it really doesn't make a lot of sense. So what can you feed your family instead? Can I suggest you try vegetable spaghetti made from swede, parsnip, pumpkin or zucchini? Veggie noodles are a fabulous alternative to pasta, with heaps of nutritional goodness and flavour. So why not give them a go? Try this recipe out if you are not convinced. I am sure it will change your mind.

GARLIC PRAWNS WITH SPAGHETTI

1 litre (4 cups) fish bone broth (for a recipe, see page 42) or salted water
2 swedes, spiralised into thin noodles
extra-virgin olive oil, to serve
lemon wedges, to serve
1 small handful of basil, chopped, to serve

Garlic prawns
4 tablespoons coconut oil or good-quality animal fat*, melted
16 raw king prawns, shelled and deveined, with tails intact
8 garlic cloves, finely sliced
2 salted anchovy fillets, rinsed and patted dry
1–2 long red chillies, deseeded and finely sliced
3 tablespoons chopped flat-leaf parsley leaves
100 ml white wine
1 x 400 g can crushed tomatoes
150 ml fish bone broth (for a recipe, see page 42) or water
sea salt and freshly ground black pepper

* See Glossary

To make the garlic prawns, melt 1 tablespoon of oil or fat in a large frying pan over medium high–heat. Add the prawns and cook on each side for 1 minute until lightly golden but not cooked all the way through, then remove from the pan. Add the remaining oil or fat, the garlic and anchovies to the pan and cook over medium heat for 30 seconds until the garlic just turns golden. Stir in the chilli and parsley and toss for 20 seconds, then pour in the wine, bring to the boil and reduce by half, about 3–4 minutes. Stir in the tomatoes and broth or water, season with salt and pepper and cook for 5 minutes until the tomatoes have broken down and the sauce is thick. Return the prawns to the pan, toss through the sauce and simmer for 1½–2 minutes until the prawns are just cooked through.

Meanwhile, bring the broth or salted water to the boil in a saucepan. Add the swede spaghetti and cook for 30 seconds until almost cooked through. Drain, reserving the broth for another use, then gently toss the spaghetti with the garlic prawns and sauce.

Arrange the spaghetti on serving plates, drizzle with a little olive oil, add a squeeze of lemon and scatter over some basil and pepper.

Serves 4

Growing up I remember smoked chicken being a 'thing'. Loads of people, including me, loved it, and smoked chicken salads were in nearly every cafe. Here, I share my simple warm salad: smoked chicken with sweet potato spirals, gently sautéed silverbeet and a delicious, easy-to-make cashew sauce. If you like, you can turn this into a cold salad by simply chilling all the cooked ingredients. And if the cashew dressing isn't your cup of tea, then you could always use a homemade mayo to bind everything together instead.

SMOKED CHICKEN, SILVERBEET & SWEET POTATO SPIRAL SALAD

2 tablespoons coconut oil or good-quality animal fat*
2 large sweet potatoes (about 700 g), spiralised into thick noodles
3 garlic cloves, chopped
4 silverbeet leaves, stalks removed and reserved for making bone broths, roughly chopped
500 g smoked chicken breast, sliced
1–2 cashew nuts (activated if possible), finely grated
extra-virgin olive oil, to serve

Cashew dressing
150 g cashew nuts
2 teaspoons lemon juice
1 garlic clove, peeled
½ teaspoon sea salt
pinch of freshly ground black pepper

* See Glossary

To make the cashew dressing, soak the cashews in 750 ml of water for 1–4 hours. Drain and rinse well. Place the cashews in the bowl of a food processor, add the lemon juice, garlic, salt and pepper and pulse until combined. Pour in 125 ml of water and process until smooth. Add more water if needed.

Place the cashew dressing in a saucepan over low heat and cook until warmed through.

Melt 1 tablespoon of coconut oil or fat in a large frying pan over medium heat. Add the sweet potato spirals and cook, tossing occasionally, for 6–8 minutes until tender. Remove from the pan and set aside.

Wipe the pan clean and place over medium heat. Melt the remaining oil in the pan, add the garlic, silverbeet and 2 tablespoons of water and sauté for 2 minutes until the silverbeet has wilted. Stir in the smoked chicken and sauté for a further minute until heated through. Add the sweet potato spirals and toss gently to combine. Season with salt and pepper to taste.

Divide the smoked chicken mixture among serving plates, spoon on some cashew dressing, sprinkle the grated cashews over the top and finish with a drizzle of olive oil.

Serves 4

This simple but mouth-watering dish of zucchini noodles with crispy chicken and a wonderful avocado dressing hits the spot each and every time. Here's to the simple things in life.

CREAMY AVOCADO WITH CHICKEN & NOODLES

4 boneless chicken thighs, skin on
2 tablespoons coconut oil or good-quality animal fat*
1 litre (4 cups) chicken bone broth (for a recipe, see page 158) or salted water
4–5 zucchini (about 700 g in total), spiralised into thin noodles
1 large handful of baby spinach leaves
80 g (½ cup) pine nuts (activated if possible), toasted, plus extra to serve
chilli flakes, to serve

Avocado sauce
2 avocados
1 handful of basil leaves
2 garlic cloves, finely chopped
4 tablespoons olive oil
3 tablespoons lemon juice
sea salt and freshly ground black pepper

* See Glossary

To make the sauce, place all the ingredients in the bowl of a food processor and blitz until smooth. Season with salt and pepper to taste.

Place the chicken between two sheets of baking paper and flatten with a mallet. Season the skin with salt.

Melt the oil or fat in a large, heavy-based frying pan over medium–high heat, add the chicken, skin-side down, and season the exposed flesh with salt. Fry the chicken, undisturbed, for 6–8 minutes until the skin is crispy and golden brown. Flip the chicken over and cook for 3 minutes until cooked through. Slice the chicken and set aside, keeping warm.

Bring the broth or salted water to the boil in a saucepan, add the zucchini noodles and cook for 20 seconds. Drain, reserving the broth for another use.

Gently mix the avocado sauce, chicken, spinach and pine nuts with the noodles. Divide between serving plates and sprinkle on some chilli flakes and a few extra pine nuts.

Serves 4

One of my favourite dishes in the world has to be pad Thai. The balance of
sweet, sour, hot and salty, together with its textural magnificence, ensure it will be a classic
for millennia to come. Usually pad Thai is served with rice noodles, but I wanted to step it
up a gear and add in some nutritional goodness in the form of spiralised swede, which is
a little like cabbage and turnip combined. If you cannot find swede, use carrot,
pumpkin or zucchini noodles, or try it with kelp noodles instead.

PAD THAI WITH CHICKEN & PRAWNS

1 tablespoon dried shrimp
3 tablespoons coconut sugar
1 tablespoon tamarind puree
2 tablespoons tamari
2 tablespoons fish sauce
2½ tablespoons coconut oil
8 raw king prawns, shelled
   and deveined with tails
   intact
2 chicken thigh fillets, finely
   sliced
4 red Asian shallots, sliced
3 eggs
1 large swede (about 500 g),
   spiralised into thick noodles
½ teaspoon chilli powder, plus
   extra to serve
150 g bean sprouts, trimmed
2 tablespoons cashew nuts
   (activated if possible),
   toasted and finely chopped
4–5 coriander sprigs, to serve
1 lime, cut into wedges

Soak the dried shrimp in water for 10 minutes, or until just
soft. Drain and pat dry. Finely chop the drained shrimp and
set aside until needed.

Put the coconut sugar, tamarind puree, tamari, fish sauce
and 2 tablespoons of water in a small bowl and mix until the
sugar dissolves.

Melt 1½ tablespoons of oil in a wok or large frying pan over
medium heat. Add the prawns, in batches, and cook on each
side for 1 minute until just cooked through, then remove from
the pan, place on a plate and cover with foil to keep warm.

Heat the remaining oil in the pan, add the chicken and cook
over medium heat for 5 minutes. Stir in the shallot and cook
for 1–2 minutes until the shallot is just starting to colour. Push
the chicken and shallot to the side of the pan. Crack in the
eggs and scramble with a fork, then push the eggs aside.

Add the swede noodles to the pan and stir-fry for 3–5 minutes,
allowing the noodles to colour a little. Pour in the tamarind
mixture, mix well and simmer for 1 minute. Add the chilli
powder and half the bean sprouts and cook for another
10 seconds. Check the seasoning.

Pile the noodle mixture onto plates and top with the remaining
bean sprouts. Serve with the cashews, coriander, lime
wedges and some extra chilli powder on the side, if desired.

Serves 2

Celeriac, revered in Mediterranean cooking for its earthy flavour, is a wonderful pasta substitute. It works well in a rich sauce, and this mushroom velouté perfectly marries the delicious, moist and tender chunks of chicken thigh (remember: the thigh is tastier than the breast) to make a family dinner that everyone will absolutely adore. If you want to add another flavour element, some free-range bacon cooked with the onion at the start takes this to another level. And, of course, adding in a handful of health-giving greens such as spinach, kale, cabbage or silverbeet at the end is a sensational idea.

CHICKEN & MUSHROOM VELOUTÉ WITH SPAGHETTI

500 ml (2 cups) chicken bone broth (for a recipe, see page 158)
3 tablespoons coconut oil or good-quality animal fat*
400 g chicken thigh fillets, cut into bite-sized pieces
1 onion, finely chopped
3 garlic cloves, finely chopped
6 field mushrooms, sliced
2 teaspoons chopped thyme
2½ tablespoons tapioca flour*
125 ml (½ cup) coconut cream
sea salt and freshly ground black pepper
Paleo Cheese (page 162), to serve
2 tablespoons finely chopped flat-leaf parsley leaves, to serve

Spaghetti
1 litre (4 cups) chicken bone broth (for a recipe, see page 158) or salted water
1½ large celeriac (about 700 g), spiralised into thin noodles

* See Glossary

Pour the broth into a saucepan and bring to a simmer.

Meanwhile, melt half the oil or fat in a saucepan over medium heat. Add the chicken and seal on all sides until golden, about 3–4 minutes, then remove from the pan. Add the remaining oil or fat and the onion and sauté for 5 minutes until the onion is soft. Add the garlic, mushrooms and thyme and sauté for a further 3 minutes until the vegetables start to colour. Mix in the tapioca flour with a wooden spoon and stir until it dissolves.

Slowly pour the hot broth into the pan, stirring constantly until the sauce comes to the boil and thickens. Stir in the coconut cream, then turn down the heat to low. Return the chicken to the pan and cook for 10 minutes until the chicken is cooked through. Season with salt and pepper.

For the spaghetti, bring the broth or salted water to the boil in a saucepan. Add the celeriac and cook for 1 minute until just tender. Drain, reserving the broth for another use.

Divide the spaghetti between serving plates, top with the chicken and mushroom velouté, grate on some paleo cheese and sprinkle over the chopped parsley.

Serves 4

Kung pao chicken is a wonderfully aromatic dish that, once eaten, is never forgotten. This is in part due to the mouth-numbing sensation of the Sichuan peppercorns, which I suggest you make a staple in your pantry, as they give Chinese dishes a unique and delicious flavour. You can substitute beef or lamb for the chicken or, for something special, try prawns or other seafood. I like to serve this with a bowl of kimchi on the side for good gut health.

KUNG PAO CHICKEN

3 tablespoons coconut oil or good-quality animal fat*
1–2 long red chillies, finely sliced
4 garlic cloves, finely chopped
2 spring onions, white part only, finely chopped
6–7 fresh shiitake mushrooms (about 100 g), sliced
4 tablespoons tamari
3 tablespoons chicken bone broth (for a recipe, see page 158) or water
2 tablespoons chilli oil (for a recipe, see page 159)
1 tablespoon coconut sugar
1 tablespoon apple cider vinegar
½ teaspoon Sichuan peppercorns, toasted and finely ground
1 tablespoon tapioca flour*, mixed with 3 tablespoons cold water
80 g (½ cup) cashew nuts (activated if possible), toasted
4–5 zucchini (about 700 g in total), spiralised into thin noodles
coriander leaves, to serve

Marinated chicken
1 tablespoon tamari
1½ teaspoons sesame oil
1 teaspoon finely grated ginger
600 g chicken thigh fillets, cut into 2 cm dice

* See Glossary

For the marinated chicken, place the tamari, sesame oil and ginger in a non-reactive bowl and mix to combine. Add the chicken and mix well to coat evenly. Cover and marinate in the refrigerator for at least 2 hours.

Melt 1 tablespoon of coconut oil or fat in a wok or large saucepan over high heat. When the oil starts to smoke, add the marinated chicken, in batches, and stir-fry for 5 minutes until golden on all sides, then transfer to a plate and set aside, keeping warm.

Wipe the pan clean, add the remaining coconut oil or fat, the chilli, garlic and spring onion and stir-fry until fragrant, about 30 seconds. Mix in 2 tablespoons of water, then add the mushrooms and cook for a further 30 seconds. Return the chicken to the pan, add the tamari, broth or water, chilli oil, coconut sugar, vinegar and Sichuan pepper and cook for 3 minutes. Stir in the tapioca paste and bring to the boil, then add the cashews and zucchini noodles and stir-fry for 30–40 seconds until the zucchini noodles are just cooked through. Scatter over the coriander leaves and serve.

Serves 4

This is a paleo twist on a simple pasta dish I enjoyed when I was a young apprentice chef. The sauce, traditionally made by combining an Italian tomato sauce with cream, is the most beautiful rose colour. Here, my dairy-free version of coconut cream and tomato passata provides the desired result. You can add any protein you like – seafood works extremely well – feel free to play around with the noodles, too. Taro can be hard to come by, so why not try zucchini, parsnip, swede, sweet potato or pumpkin?

FETTUCCINE WITH CHICKEN & BACON ROSA SAUCE

1 tablespoon coconut oil or good-quality animal fat*
4 slices of rindless bacon, chopped
600 g chicken thigh fillets, cut into bite-sized pieces
1 onion, finely chopped
3 garlic cloves, finely chopped
1–2 long red chillies, deseeded and finely chopped (leave the seeds in if you like it extra spicy)
100 ml white wine (such as chardonnay)
450 g tomato passata
200 ml coconut cream
100 ml chicken bone broth (for a recipe, see page 158)
250 g cherry tomatoes, halved
1 large taro, spiralised into thick noodles
sea salt and freshly ground black pepper
chopped flat-leaf parsley leaves, to serve
extra-virgin olive oil, to serve

* See Glossary

Melt the coconut oil or fat in a large frying pan over medium–high heat. Add the bacon and fry until golden and crispy, 5–6 minutes, then remove and transfer to a plate.

Add the chicken to the pan and cook for 2 minutes on all sides until golden, then remove from the pan. Reduce the heat to medium, add the onion to the pan and sauté for 5–6 minutes until soft. Stir in the garlic and chilli and cook for 1 minute until fragrant.

Return the bacon and chicken to the pan, pour in the wine and reduce by half. Pour in the passata, coconut cream and broth and reduce the heat to low. Simmer, stirring occasionally, for 15 minutes until the sauce has thickened slightly.

Mix the cherry tomatoes into the sauce, then fold in the taro fettuccine and cook for 6–8 minutes until the fettuccine is cooked through. Season with salt and pepper. Place on a serving platter or divide among serving plates, sprinkle on some parsley and drizzle with a little extra-virgin olive oil.

Serves 4

Everyone loves a good chicken and cashew stir-fry and this one, I know,
will become a family favourite. I've upped the veggie intake to make this a meal to
strengthen and nourish. To mix it up, play around with different proteins like prawns,
scallops, wild-caught fish or free-range pork. If cashews aren't your thing,
simply substitute macadamias or sesame seeds.

CHICKEN & CASHEW STIR-FRY

3 tablespoons tamari
2 tablespoons honey or
coconut sugar
1½ tablespoons fish sauce
6 chicken thigh fillets, cut into
bite-sized pieces
2 tablespoons coconut oil
1 onion, chopped
4 garlic cloves, sliced
5 cm piece of ginger, julienned
1 lemongrass stalk, white part
only, finely chopped
1–2 long red chillies,
deseeded and sliced, plus
extra to serve
1 bunch of broccolini (about
180 g), roughly chopped
1 bunch of choy sum (about
230 g), roughly chopped
155 g (1 cup) cashew nuts
(activated if possible),
toasted
4–5 carrots, spiralised into thin
noodles
1 zucchini, spiralised into thin
noodles
125 ml (½ cup) chicken bone
broth (for a recipe, see
page 158)
1 tablespoon apple cider
vinegar
sea salt and freshly ground
black pepper
1 handful of coriander leaves
lime wedges, to serve
(optional)

Place the tamari, honey or sugar and fish sauce in a
bowl, add the chicken and mix well. Leave to marinate for
5 minutes.

Meanwhile, melt the coconut oil in a wok or large frying pan
over medium–high heat and swirl around the pan. Add the
onion, garlic, ginger, lemongrass and chilli and cook, stirring
frequently, for 2–3 minutes until soft and fragrant.

Add the chicken and marinade to the pan and sauté for
5 minutes. Stir in the broccolini, choy sum, cashews and
carrot and zucchini noodles and toss together. Pour in the
broth and vinegar and cook for 3 minutes until the vegetables
are soft and the chicken is cooked through. If the stir-fry is
looking a little dry, mix in some water. Season with salt and
pepper if needed.

Leave the stir-fry in the pan or place on a platter. Sprinkle with
the coriander and serve with the lime wedges (if using) and
the extra chilli on the side.

Serves 4

I absolutely adore this aromatic curry sauce that creates a wonderful pool for the chicken and vegetables to bathe in. Here, I have teamed the curry with one of my all-time favourite vegetables, the humble pumpkin. Spiralised into noodles, the pumpkin is perfect for slurping down while you enjoy your curry. Carrot, sweet potato and zucchini noodles also work well, as do kelp noodles. And feel free to swap out the chicken for duck, prawns, beef or mussels.

THAI RED CHICKEN & PUMPKIN CURRY

3 tablespoons coconut oil
1 onion, chopped
2 tablespoons red curry paste
2 garlic cloves, finely chopped
700 g chicken thigh fillets, cut into 2.5 cm pieces
1 teaspoon coconut sugar or honey
1 x 400 ml can coconut milk
300 g broccoli, trimmed and broken into florets
4 Japanese eggplants, cut into 2 cm pieces
a splash of fish sauce, plus extra if needed
zest and juice of ½ lime
1 litre (4 cups) chicken bone broth (for a recipe, see page 158) or salted water
600 g butternut pumpkin, spiralised into thin noodles
1 large handful of Thai basil leaves, to serve
1 bird's eye chilli, finely sliced, to serve (optional)

Melt the oil in a saucepan over medium–low heat. Add the onion and cook for 5–6 minutes until soft. Stir in the curry paste and garlic and cook, stirring occasionally, for 2 minutes until fragrant and the oil separates and comes to the surface. Next, add the chicken and cook for 2–3 minutes, then mix in the coconut sugar or honey and coconut milk. Bring to the boil and simmer for 10 minutes. Add the broccoli and eggplant and cook for a further 10 minutes until the veggies are just tender and the chicken is cooked through. Season with a splash of fish sauce and the lime juice.

Bring the broth or salted water to the boil in a large saucepan. Add the pumpkin noodles and blanch for about 50–60 seconds until almost cooked through. Drain, reserving the broth for another use.

To serve, divide the pumpkin noodles between serving bowls. Ladle over the chicken, vegetables and sauce, scatter on the lime zest and serve with the basil and chilli (if using).

Serves 4

I enjoy creating dishes I know everyone will love. And one look at this schnitzel roll will have the whole family lining up to tuck into its mouth-watering goodness. Paleo rolls and a grain-free coating for the schnitzel make this a completely grain- and dairy-free adventure. Feel free to go to town with your spiraliser: carrot, cucumber, beetroot and daikon make exciting fillings.

CHICKEN SCHNITZEL ROLL WITH SPICY AIOLI

4 chicken thigh fillets
200 g almond meal, plus extra if needed
1 teaspoon garlic powder
1 teaspoon onion powder
½ teaspoon chilli powder
2 teaspoons dried parsley
sea salt and freshly ground black pepper
60 g tapioca flour*
3 eggs
4 tablespoons coconut milk
400 ml coconut oil
4 slices of rindless bacon
4 Nut-free Bread Rolls (page 162)
4 cos lettuce leaves
1 large carrot, spiralised into thick noodles
1 avocado, finely sliced

Spicy aioli
4 heaped tablespoons aioli (for a recipe, see page 157)
1½ teaspoons sriracha chilli sauce (for a recipe, see page 165), plus extra if needed

* See Glossary

Place the chicken between two sheets of baking paper and flatten with a mallet until 1 cm thick.

Combine the almond meal, dried spices and herbs in a shallow bowl and mix well. Season with salt and pepper and set aside. Place the tapioca flour in another shallow bowl. In a third bowl, whisk the eggs and coconut milk to combine.

Dust the chicken with the tapioca flour, shaking off any excess. Working with one piece at a time, dip the chicken in the egg mixture, then evenly coat with the almond meal mixture.

Heat 390 ml of coconut oil in a large, deep frying pan over medium–high heat to 160°C. (To test, place a tiny piece of chicken in the oil – if it starts to bubble around the chicken immediately, the oil is ready.) Shallow fry the crumbed chicken, in batches, for 3–5 minutes on both sides, or until golden and cooked through. Remove from the pan and drain on paper towel. Season with salt and pepper and set aside until needed.

Melt the remaining oil in another frying pan over medium heat. Add the bacon and fry on each side for 3 minutes until lightly golden and crisp. Set aside, keeping warm.

To make the spicy aioli, combine the aioli and sriracha in a bowl, adding a little more sriracha if you like it extra spicy.

Cut the rolls in half, place a cos leaf on each base, then add the carrot noodles, schnitzel, avocado, bacon and a dollop of spicy aioli. Top with the other half of the roll and serve.

Serves 4

The whole family will adore the flavours in this dish and, once tried, will be asking for it to make a regular appearance at the dinner table. Any leftovers are perfect to take to school or work for lunch the next day. Get the kids involved with the preparation. They will love to help make the dressing or vegetable spirals.

BANG BANG CHICKEN

600 g boneless chicken thighs, skin on
2 tablespoons coconut oil or good-quality animal fat*
sea salt and freshly ground black pepper
2 Lebanese cucumbers, spiralised into thick noodles
2 carrots, spiralised into thin noodles
6 butter lettuce leaves, roughly chopped
2 radishes, julienned
2 spring onions, sliced diagonally
1 large handful of coriander leaves, plus extra to serve

Sesame sauce
1 teaspoon Sichuan peppercorns
2 tablespoons coconut sugar
2 tablespoons tamari
2 tablespoons apple cider vinegar
70 g hulled tahini
1 tablespoon sesame oil
1 teaspoon white sesame seeds, toasted
1 teaspoon chilli oil (for a recipe, see page 159), plus extra to serve

* See Glossary

Coat the chicken with half the oil or fat and season with a generous amount of salt and pepper.

Melt the remaining oil in a frying pan over medium–high heat. Add the chicken and cook for 4 minutes on each side until golden and cooked through. Remove from the heat and rest for a couple of minutes, before slicing and covering with foil to keep warm.

To make the sesame sauce, toast the Sichuan peppercorns in a frying pan over medium heat until fragrant, about 1 minute. Use a mortar and pestle or a spice grinder to finely grind the peppercorns. Transfer to a bowl, add the remaining ingredients and 1 tablespoon of water and mix well.

Combine the cucumber and carrot noodles, lettuce, radish, spring onion and coriander in a bowl, pour on half the sesame sauce and gently toss. Season with salt and pepper if needed. Arrange on a platter, top with the chicken, drizzle on the remaining sesame sauce, scatter over the extra coriander leaves and serve with some extra chilli oil on the side.

Serves 2–3

MEAT

We all love a good meatball dish and this one will make every parent happy. The meatballs are teamed with an abundance of vegetables that look so pretty on the plate kids won't be able to resist them. If the kids are not that pumped about olives, simply add them to yours with some extra chilli flakes to make this nice and spicy, which is how I love to eat it. Mmm, I'm getting hungry and I have some mince in the fridge … time to cook!

SPICY ITALIAN PORK MEATBALLS

2 tablespoons coconut oil or good-quality animal fat*
1 red onion, sliced
1 red capsicum, finely sliced
4 cloves Garlic Confit (page 160), crushed
2 carrots, spiralised into thin noodles
155 g (1 cup) pitted kalamata olives, halved
125 ml (½ cup) beef or chicken bone broth (for a recipe, see pages 157–8) or water
150 g silverbeet, stalks removed and leaves finely shredded
2 zucchini, spiralised into thin noodles
1 teaspoon chilli flakes, or to taste
extra-virgin olive oil, to serve

Pork meatballs
500 g pork mince
3 cloves Garlic Confit (page 160), crushed
1 teaspoon chilli flakes
1½ teaspoons fennel seeds, toasted and coarsely ground
1¼ teaspoons sea salt
½ teaspoon freshly ground black pepper
3 tablespoons tallow or pork lard*
1 tablespoon chopped flat-leaf parsley leaves, plus extra to serve

* See Glossary

To make the pork meatballs, combine all the ingredients in a bowl and mix well. Roll into walnut-sized balls and place on a plate.

Melt the coconut oil or fat in a large frying pan over medium–high heat. Add the meatballs, in batches, and cook for 3 minutes on all sides until browned and almost cooked through. Remove from the pan, set aside on a plate and cover with foil to keep warm.

Reduce the heat to medium, add the onion and capsicum to the pan and sauté for 6 minutes until soft. Increase the heat to medium–high, add the confit garlic cloves, the carrot noodles and olives and sauté for 30 seconds. Pour in the broth or water, bring to the boil and cook for 2–3 minutes until the carrot is tender. Add the silverbeet and zucchini and toss for 1 minute until the zucchini is almost cooked through. Return the meatballs to the pan, add the chilli flakes and cook for 1 minute, then remove from the heat and season with salt and pepper. Transfer to a platter or serving plates, drizzle on some extra-virgin olive oil and serve.

Serves 4

One look at this salad will have your family or guests picking their jaws up off the floor. And the best thing is that you can have this ready in about 20 minutes, or even less if you have helpers in the kitchen. You could substitute the beef for a lovely piece of tuna or some prawns.

JAPANESE BEEF SALAD WITH PONZU & SESAME DRESSING

1 x 600 g beef eye fillet, trimmed and cut in half lengthways
3 tablespoons dried wakame*
2 tablespoons coconut oil, melted
sea salt and freshly ground black pepper
1 Lebanese cucumber, spiralised into thin noodles
¼ daikon, spiralised into thin noodles
1 large carrot, spiralised into thin noodles
2 spring onions, finely sliced
2 handfuls of baby spinach
150 g cherry tomatoes, halved
baby snow pea sprouts, to serve
black and white sesame seeds, toasted, to serve

Onion ponzu
½ onion, very finely chopped
1 garlic clove, finely chopped
3 tablespoons olive oil or macadamia oil
1 tablespoon lemon juice
3 tablespoons apple cider vinegar
2 tablespoons tamari
½ teaspoon finely grated ginger

Sesame dressing
2 tablespoons hulled tahini
2 tablespoons tamari
1 teaspoon apple cider vinegar
1 teaspoon honey
1 teaspoon sesame oil

* See Glossary

Remove the beef from the fridge 15 minutes before cooking to bring it to room temperature.

Place the wakame in a bowl, cover with cold water and set aside for 20 minutes. Drain well.

To make the onion ponzu, combine all the ingredients in a bowl and set aside.

To make the sesame dressing, mix the tahini with 3 tablespoons of water in a small serving bowl, then stir in the tamari, vinegar, honey and sesame oil. Set aside until needed.

Heat the barbecue to hot. Lightly brush the beef fillet with the coconut oil and season with salt and pepper. Sear the beef on all sides for 1½ minutes, or until cooked to your liking. Rest the beef in a warm place for 4 minutes.

Finely slice the beef and place on a platter with the vegetable noodles, spring onion, wakame, spinach, cherry tomatoes and sprouts. Drizzle on a few tablespoons of onion ponzu, then drizzle on some sesame dressing. Scatter over some sesame seeds and serve with the remaining dressing on the side.

Serves 4

On a cool winter's evening, nothing can be more comforting and warming than a slowly cooked lamb ragu. Here we embrace real food and serve the ragu with a parsnip pappardelle. This bowl of goodness will make you feel calmly content.

LAMB RAGU WITH PAPPARDELLE

4 tablespoons coconut oil or good-quality animal fat*
1 onion, finely chopped
1 carrot, finely chopped
1 celery stalk, finely chopped
4 garlic cloves, finely chopped
1 tablespoon finely chopped rosemary leaves
800 g boneless lamb shoulder, cut into 2.5 cm cubes
200 ml red wine (such as shiraz)
500 ml (2 cups) beef or chicken bone broth (for a recipe, see pages 157–8) or water
2 x 400 g cans whole peeled tomatoes
1 teaspoon chilli flakes
sea salt and freshly ground black pepper
5–6 parsnips (about 850 g), spiralised into ribbons
lemon-infused extra-virgin olive oil, to serve
1 tablespoon finely chopped flat-leaf parsley leaves

* See Glossary

Melt 2 tablespoons of coconut oil or fat in a large, heavy-based saucepan over medium heat. Add the onion, carrot and celery and sauté for 7 minutes until the vegetables are starting to caramelise. Stir in the garlic and rosemary and continue to cook for 1 minute until fragrant, then remove from the pan.

Increase the heat to medium–high and melt the remaining coconut oil or fat in the pan. Add the lamb and cook for 2 minutes on each side until browned. Pour in the wine, bring to the boil and reduce by half, about 3 minutes. Return the cooked vegetables to the pan, add the broth or water, the tomatoes and chilli flakes and bring to the boil. Reduce the heat to low, cover with a lid and simmer gently for 3 hours until the meat is tender and falling apart. Season with salt and pepper.

Gently mix the parsnip ribbons into the hot lamb ragu and cook for 2–3 minutes until the parsnip is cooked through. Arrange on serving plates or in a serving dish, drizzle over a little lemon-infused olive oil and sprinkle on the parsley.

Serves 4–6

This cauliflower alfredo sauce will be a welcome addition to your cooking repertoire.
I love the bacon that is added to this sauce. If you want something a little heartier,
feel free to use parsnip instead of zucchini for the spaghetti.

CAULIFLOWER ALFREDO
WITH SPAGHETTI

2 teaspoons coconut oil
2 slices of rindless bacon,
  finely chopped
4–5 zucchini (about 700 g
  in total), spiralised into
  thick noodles
2 tablespoons finely chopped
  flat-leaf parsley leaves, plus
  extra to serve
extra-virgin olive oil, to serve

Alfredo sauce
1 tablespoon coconut oil or
  good-quality animal fat*
4 garlic cloves, finely chopped
350 ml beef or chicken bone
  broth (for a recipe, see
  pages 157–8) or water, plus
  extra if needed
½ head of cauliflower (about
  500 g), chopped
sea salt and freshly ground
  black pepper

* See Glossary

To make the alfredo sauce, melt the oil or fat in a saucepan over medium heat. Add the garlic and sauté for 30 seconds until fragrant. Pour in the broth or water, add the cauliflower and bring to the boil. Cover with a lid, turn the heat down to low and simmer, stirring occasionally, for 15–20 minutes until the cauliflower is very soft. Blend with a hand-held blender until smooth and creamy. If the sauce is too thick, add more broth or water. Season with salt and pepper and set aside, keeping warm.

Melt the coconut oil in a large frying pan over medium heat. Add the bacon and sauté until golden and crispy, about 5–6 minutes. Add the zucchini spaghetti and cook for 1–1½ minutes until almost cooked through. Remove from the heat, pour in the sauce, add the parsley and gently mix to combine. Season with salt and pepper if needed. Drizzle over some extra-virgin olive oil, scatter over the extra chopped parsley and serve.

Serves 4

This dish will have the whole family singing your praises! The homemade sauces may take a little time, but if you make up big batches of each you'll always have them in the fridge. The tortillas are awesome and also work well instead of naan in Indian dishes.

PULLED LAMB TACOS

1 x 1 kg boneless lamb shoulder, trimmed of sinew
3 tablespoons coconut oil or good-quality animal fat*, melted
sea salt and freshly ground black pepper
3 tablespoons maple syrup
2 tablespoons garlic powder
½ teaspoon mustard powder
2 tablespoons onion powder
½ teaspoon freshly ground white pepper
125 ml (½ cup) barbecue sauce (for a recipe, see page 157), plus extra to serve
125 ml (½ cup) Worcestershire sauce (for a recipe, see page 165)
1 large carrot, spiralised into thin noodles, to serve
Coleslaw (page 66), to serve
coriander leaves, to serve
lime wedges, to serve

Chipotle aioli
250 g aioli (for a recipe, see page 157)
2 chipotles in adobo sauce*, or to taste
1 tablespoon adobo sauce

Coconut flour tortillas
3 tablespoons coconut flour
3 tablespoons arrowroot*
¼ teaspoon baking powder
½ teaspoon fine sea salt
8 large eggwhites
2 tablespoons coconut oil

* See Glossary

Preheat the oven to 150°C. Lightly grease a roasting tin.

Cut the lamb into three even pieces, then rub with 1 tablespoon of oil or fat. Sprinkle with salt and pepper.

Melt the remaining oil or fat in a large, heavy-based frying pan over high heat. Add the lamb and sear for 2 minutes on all sides until lightly browned. Remove from the pan and place, fat-side up, in the prepared tin.

Combine the maple syrup, garlic powder, mustard powder, onion powder, white pepper, barbecue sauce, Worcestershire sauce and 800 ml of water in a bowl. Pour over the lamb, cover the tin tightly with a double layer of foil and roast in the oven for 1 hour. Reduce the oven temperature to 100°C and continue to roast for 6–7 hours, or until the lamb is very tender. Remove the lamb, reserving the liquid. Shred the lamb, adding some of the reserved liquid to moisten, and season with salt and pepper, if needed.

To make the chipotle aioli, combine all the ingredients in a jug and blend until smooth using a hand-held blender. (Leftover aioli will keep in an airtight container in the fridge for 4–5 days.)

To make the tortillas, whisk the coconut flour, arrowroot, baking powder, salt, eggwhites and 125 ml of water in a large bowl to make a smooth batter. Melt 1 teaspoon of oil in a small frying pan over medium–high heat. Pour about 3 tablespoons of batter into the pan, slightly tilting and swirling the pan to spread the batter out to form a thin tortilla, about 13 cm in diameter. Cook for a few minutes, or until golden brown, then flip and cook the other side until lightly golden. Transfer to a plate and keep warm. Repeat until you have eight tortillas.

To serve, top each tortilla with some carrot, coleslaw and pulled lamb, spoon over a little chipotle aioli, drizzle over some extra barbecue sauce and finish with the coriander leaves and a squeeze of lime.

Serves 4–6

This is the most ambitious dish in the whole book and the one I love the most. I always try to pop a couple of recipes in my books that challenge home cooks to try something new. So give this delicious curry a whirl to see just how amazing bone marrow can be.

MASSAMAN CURRY WITH THAI NOODLE SALAD

2 tablespoons coconut oil or good-quality animal fat*
1 onion, finely chopped
3 tablespoons Massaman Curry Paste (page 160)
3 kaffir lime leaves, torn
1 cinnamon stick
3 tablespoons coconut cream
1 x 400 g can crushed tomatoes
250 ml (1 cup) beef bone broth (for a recipe, see page 157)
2 teaspoons tamarind paste
2 teaspoons coconut sugar
1½ teaspoons fish sauce
1 kg bone marrow, cut lengthways into 5 cm pieces (ask your butcher to do this)
sea salt and freshly ground black pepper

Thai noodle salad
1 carrot, spiralised into thin noodles
1 Lebanese cucumber, spiralised into thin noodles
¼ daikon, spiralised into thin noodles
1 handful of mixed Vietnamese mint, Thai basil and coriander leaves
1 long red chilli, finely sliced
4 tablespoons Nam Jim Dressing (page 161)

To serve
Cauliflower Rice (page 158)
Paleo Roti Bread (page 163)
roughly chopped cashew nuts
lime wedges

* See Glossary

Preheat the oven to 200°C.

Melt the oil or fat in a large frying pan over medium–high heat. Add the onion and sauté for 5–6 minutes until soft, then add the curry paste, lime leaves and cinnamon and cook for 2 minutes until fragrant and the paste starts to separate. Mix in the coconut cream, tomatoes, broth, tamarind, coconut sugar and fish sauce. Bring to a simmer, reduce the heat to low and cook for 30 minutes until the sauce is thick and full of flavour.

Meanwhile, season the bone marrow with salt and pepper, place on a baking tray and roast in the oven for 12 minutes until starting to brown.

Add the roasted bone marrow to the pan, stir to coat with the curry sauce and simmer for 5 minutes.

To make the salad, place the vegetable noodles in a bowl, add the herbs, chilli and nam jim dressing and gently mix to combine.

Sprinkle the massaman curry with cashew nuts and serve it with the noodle salad, some cauliflower rice, roti and lime wedges on the side.

Serves 4

TIP

If bone marrow is not your thing, try beef cheeks, oxtail, gravy beef or lamb shanks instead.

To the purist, a classic carbonara is all about the black pepper, bacon and egg yolk folded in to bind everything together. Luckily, I am not that much of a purist. I like to mix things up a little, which is why I created this recipe. It combines two other wonderful ingredients that work well with bacon and egg: pumpkin and sage.
Tossed with parsnip fettuccine, this works a treat.

PUMPKIN CARBONARA
WITH FETTUCCINE

2 tablespoons coconut oil or
  good-quality animal fat*
350 g rindless bacon, cut into
  5 mm dice
1 onion, chopped
2 garlic cloves, chopped
700 g butternut pumpkin,
  cut into 2 cm dice
1.5 litres (6 cups) chicken
  bone broth (for a recipe, see
  page 158)
100 ml coconut cream
1 egg
freshly ground black pepper
4–5 parsnips (about 600 g),
  spiralised into thick noodles

Crispy sage leaves
4 tablespoons coconut oil or
  good-quality animal fat*
20 g (1 cup) sage leaves
sea salt

* See Glossary

To make the crispy sage leaves, melt the oil or fat in a small saucepan over medium heat. Cooking in batches of four at a time, fry the sage leaves for 3–4 seconds until crisp. Remove with a slotted spoon and drain on paper towel. Season with salt and set aside.

Melt the oil or fat in a non-stick frying pan over medium heat. Add the bacon and cook, stirring occasionally, until golden and crisp, about 8 minutes. Remove the bacon and keep warm. Add the onion to the pan and cook, stirring occasionally, for 5–6 minutes until soft. Add the garlic and cook for 30 seconds until fragrant. Stir in the pumpkin, pour in 500 ml of broth and cover with a lid. Bring to the boil, then reduce the heat to low and simmer until the pumpkin is very soft and the liquid has been absorbed, about 15–20 minutes. Mix in the coconut cream and egg and blend with a hand-blender until smooth and creamy. Season with salt and pepper.

Bring the remaining broth to the boil in a large saucepan. Add the parsnip noodles and blanch for 50–60 seconds until almost cooked through. Drain, reserving the broth for another use.

Combine the noodles, pumpkin puree and bacon and gently mix. Serve on plates, topped with the crispy sage leaves and sprinkled with pepper.

Serves 4

Here is a very simple tomato-based 'pasta' dish that has all the usual suspects: prosciutto, olives, rocket and a lovely tomato sauce tossed with parsnip fettuccine. Feel free to play around with your favourite pasta sauce ingredients and substitute or add as you please. Remember: there are no rules when it comes to creating fabulous home-cooked meals.

PROSCIUTTO, TOMATO & OLIVE FETTUCCINE

2 tablespoons coconut oil or good-quality animal fat*
1 onion, finely chopped
4 garlic cloves, finely chopped
1 tablespoon tomato paste
125 ml (½ cup) white wine (such as chardonnay)
150 g pitted kalamata olives
3 tomatoes, deseeded and cut into 1 cm dice
1 tablespoon finely chopped flat-leaf parsley leaves
4 tablespoons olive oil
sea salt and freshly ground black pepper
1 litre (4 cups) chicken bone broth (for a recipe, see page 158) or salted water
4–5 parsnips (about 700 g), spiralised into thin noodles
200 g finely sliced prosciutto, torn
1–2 large handfuls of rocket leaves, chopped
chilli flakes, to serve
lemon wedges, to serve (optional)

* See Glossary

Melt the coconut oil or fat in a non-stick frying pan over medium heat. Add the onion and cook for 5–6 minutes until soft. Stir in the garlic and cook for 30 seconds until fragrant, then mix in the tomato paste and cook for 1 minute. Pour in the wine, bring to the boil and reduce the liquid by half, about 3 minutes. Add the olives, tomato and parsley and simmer for 1–1½ minutes until the tomato is soft. Remove from the heat, stir in the olive oil and season with salt and pepper.

Meanwhile, bring the broth or salted water to the boil in a large saucepan. Add the parsnip fettuccine and cook for 30 seconds, or until the noodles are almost cooked through. Drain, reserving the broth for another use.

Mix the fettuccine into the sauce until evenly coated, then place on serving plates. Top with the prosciutto and rocket leaves, sprinkle on some pepper and chilli flakes and serve with lemon wedges on the side, if desired.

Serves 4

For everyone out there who loves a good beef ragu but can't tolerate tomatoes, I have created this wonderful bolognese. The nomato sauce uses beetroot instead of tomato, which gives this dish a wonderful purple colour along with some earthiness and sweetness. Serve with any type of spiralised vegetable or try it with kelp noodles.

NOMATO SPAGHETTI BOLOGNESE

3 tablespoons coconut oil or good-quality animal fat*
½ onion, finely chopped
3 garlic cloves, finely chopped
600 g beef mince
500 ml (2 cups) Nomato Sauce (page 161)
1 teaspoon dried oregano
1.25 litres (5 cups) chicken bone broth (for a recipe, see page 158)
sea salt
5 zucchini (about 600 g), spiralised into thin noodles
a splash of olive oil
1 small handful of basil or flat-leaf parsley leaves, chopped

* See Glossary

Melt 2 tablespoons of coconut oil or fat in a large frying pan over medium heat. Add the onion and garlic and cook, stirring, for 5 minutes until soft. Add the beef and cook, stirring with a wooden spoon to break up any lumps, for 5 minutes until browned. Stir in the nomato sauce, oregano, 250 ml of broth and a good pinch of salt, reduce the heat to low and simmer, stirring occasionally, for 20 minutes. Add a little more broth if the sauce is too thick.

Bring the remaining broth to the boil in a saucepan. Add the zucchini spaghetti and cook for 30 seconds until tender. Drain, reserving the broth for another use. Toss the spaghetti with the olive oil and season with salt.

Divide the spaghetti between four serving bowls, spoon on the bolognese sauce, sprinkle with the basil or parsley and serve with vegetables or a salad.

Serves 4

My family loves a Chinese stir-fry as a mid-week cook up. And the best news about my black pepper beef is that it takes only 20 minutes to get it on the table. The amount of crushed black pepper used here may seem like a lot, but it is actually the star of this dish, so don't skimp on it.

BLACK PEPPER BEEF

1 kg beef eye fillet or sirloin, cut into 2 cm cubes

3 tablespoons coconut oil or good-quality animal fat*

4 spring onions, green and white parts separated and chopped

3 garlic cloves, finely chopped

1 red capsicum, roughly chopped

1 choy sum, roughly chopped

2½ teaspoons black peppercorns, finely crushed

3 tablespoons honey

2 teaspoons apple cider vinegar

4 tablespoons tamari

4 tablespoons chicken bone broth (for a recipe, see page 158) or water

1 teaspoon sesame oil

2 teaspoons grated ginger

2 tablespoons tapioca flour*, mixed with 2 tablespoons cold water

2 carrots, spiralised into thin noodles

2 zucchini, spiralised into thin noodles

* See Glossary

Heat a wok or large, deep frying pan over high heat until it just begins to smoke. Add 2 tablespoons of coconut oil or fat and swirl around the pan. Tip in the beef, in batches, and stir-fry until browned, about 2–3 minutes, then remove from the pan. Melt the remaining coconut oil or fat in the pan and reduce the heat to medium–high. Add the white part of the spring onion, the garlic, capsicum and choy sum and stir-fry for 2 minutes until just tender. Sprinkle on the pepper and cook for 10 seconds until fragrant, then mix in the honey, vinegar, tamari, broth or water, sesame oil, ginger and tapioca paste and bring to the boil. Add the carrot noodles and cook for another minute.

Return the beef to the pan and toss with the sauce and veggies. Add the zucchini noodles and the remaining spring onion, gently toss and cook for 1 minute until heated through. Place on a large platter or individual plates and serve.

Serves 4

In this dish I simply add cooked spiced lamb meatballs to my delicious and very popular Moroccan carrot salad and then finish it off with a yummy tahini dressing. Enjoy!

MIDDLE EASTERN LAMB MEATBALL SALAD

1 tablespoon coconut oil or good-quality animal fat*
4 tablespoons extra-virgin olive oil
1 tablespoon lemon juice
1 tablespoon apple cider vinegar
1 tablespoon honey
1 teaspoon finely grated ginger
1 long red chilli, deseeded and finely chopped (optional)
½ teaspoon ground sumac, plus extra for sprinkling
4 large carrots (about 500 g), spiralised into thin noodles
1 handful of almonds (activated if possible), toasted and chopped
1 large handful of coriander leaves, chopped
1 handful of mint leaves, chopped
3 tablespoons dried barberries* or currants
140 g Tahini & Yoghurt Dressing (page 165)

Meatballs
400 g lamb mince
2 garlic cloves, finely chopped
1½ teaspoons pomegranate molasses
1 tablespoon chopped flat-leaf parsley leaves
2 teaspoons Turkish Spice Mix (page 165)
sea salt and freshly ground black pepper

* See Glossary

To make the meatballs, combine the lamb, garlic, pomegranate molasses, parsley and Turkish spices in a bowl, mix thoroughly and season with salt and pepper. With wet hands, shape the lamb mixture into walnut-sized balls.

Melt the coconut oil or fat in a large, non-stick frying pan over medium heat. Add the meatballs and cook for 2–3 minutes until browned all over and just cooked through. Remove from the heat and set aside, keeping warm.

Whisk together the olive oil, lemon juice, vinegar, honey and ginger in a large bowl. Add the chilli (if using), sumac, carrot, almonds, coriander, mint, barberries or currants and meatballs. Toss and season with salt and pepper.

Arrange the salad on a platter. Spoon the tahini and yoghurt dressing into a small bowl. Sprinkle some extra sumac over the dressing and the salad. Serve the salad with the dressing on the side.

Serves 4

If you have never tried this classic Korean dish, then give it a go – it's really quite simple. My advice is to make a lot, as once this goes on the table your family will be sure to ask for more.

BIBIMBAP

3 tablespoons dried wakame*
1 spring onion, julienned
150 g kimchi
sriracha chilli sauce (for a
    recipe, see page 165)
2 cups Cauliflower Rice
    (page 158)
4 egg yolks
white and black sesame seeds,
    toasted, to serve

Seasoned bean sprouts
250 g bean sprouts, trimmed
½ teaspoon sea salt
1 tablespoon white sesame
    seeds, toasted
1 tablespoon sesame oil

Seasoned carrots
1 teaspoon coconut oil
3 carrots, spiralised into
    thin noodles
½ teaspoon sea salt
1 tablespoon sesame oil

Seasoned cucumber
1 Lebanese cucumber,
    spiralised into thin noodles
½ teaspoon sea salt

Seasoned daikon
¼ daikon, spiralised into
    thin noodles
½ teaspoon sea salt

Seasoned beef
500 g beef eye fillet or sirloin,
    cut into thin strips
2 garlic cloves, finely chopped
2 tablespoons tamari
1 tablespoon honey
5 teaspoons coconut oil
sea salt and freshly ground
    black pepper
½ teaspoon sesame oil

* See Glossary

Place the wakame in a bowl, cover with cold water and set aside for 20 minutes. Drain well.

For the seasoned bean sprouts, combine 125 ml of water with the bean sprouts and salt in a saucepan and bring to the boil. Reduce the heat to low, cover and simmer for 5 minutes. Drain and transfer the sprouts to a bowl. Mix with the sesame seeds and sesame oil, then set aside.

For the seasoned carrots, melt the coconut oil in a frying pan over medium heat. Add the carrot and salt and stir-fry for 30 seconds until just tender. Drizzle with the sesame oil, transfer to a bowl and set aside.

For the seasoned cucumber, place the cucumber and salt in a large bowl, toss well and set aside for 5 minutes. Gently squeeze the cucumber to remove any excess liquid. Transfer to another bowl and set aside.

For the seasoned daikon, place the daikon and salt in a large bowl, toss well and set aside.

For the seasoned beef, combine the beef, garlic, tamari, honey and 1 teaspoon of the coconut oil in a bowl and mix well. Set aside to marinate for 15 minutes. Place the remaining coconut oil in a wok or large saucepan over medium–high heat. Add the beef and marinade and stir-fry for 2 minutes. Season with salt and pepper if needed. Transfer to a bowl and top with the sesame oil.

Place the wakame, spring onion, kimchi and sriracha in small individual bowls.

Divide the cauliflower rice among four serving bowls, top with the seasoned salads, the beef and an egg yolk, sprinkle on the sesame seeds and serve with the wakame, spring onion, kimchi and sriracha on the side.

Serves 4

To me, bolognese is all about comfort food and childhood memories, and while I know this isn't really a standard bolognese, I wanted to create an equally memorable meal for you and your family. So spread your wings, try this Chinese-inspired version and fill your kitchen with wonderful aromas. I have teamed this with parsnip noodles, as they are simply divine, but zucchini, carrot, pumpkin or even kelp noodles also work well.

CHINESE BOLOGNESE WITH NOODLES

2 tablespoons coconut oil or good-quality animal fat*
3 red Asian shallots, finely chopped
1–2 long red chillies, deseeded and sliced
3 garlic cloves, finely chopped
1 teaspoon finely grated ginger
2 spring onions, white and green parts separated, finely sliced
600 g pork mince
1½ tablespoons sriracha chilli sauce (for a recipe, see page 165)
2 tablespoons Paleo Hoisin Sauce (page 163)
3 tablespoons tamari
1 teaspoon coconut sugar
185 ml (¾ cup) beef or chicken bone broth (for a recipe, see pages 157–8), plus extra if needed
2 teaspoons tapioca flour*, mixed with 2 tablespoons water
1 teaspoon sesame oil
1 handful of coriander leaves

Parsnip noodles
1 litre (4 cups) beef or chicken bone broth (for a recipe, see pages 157–8) or salted water
4–5 parsnips (about 700 g), spiralised into thick noodles

* See Glossary

Melt the coconut oil or fat in a wok or large, deep frying pan over high heat. Add the shallot and sauté for 2 minutes until translucent. Mix in the chilli, garlic, ginger and the white part of the spring onion and fry for 30 seconds until soft. Add the pork and stir-fry for 5–6 minutes, breaking up any lumps with a wooden spoon. Stir in the sriracha and hoisin sauces, tamari, coconut sugar, broth, tapioca paste and sesame oil and bring to the boil. Turn the heat down to low and simmer for 10 minutes until slightly thickened. Mix in more broth if the mixture is too dry.

For the parsnip noodles, bring the broth or salted water to the boil in a saucepan. Add the noodles and cook for 1–2 minutes until tender. Drain, reserving the broth for another use.

Spoon the noodles onto serving plates, top with the sauce and sprinkle on the remaining spring onion and the coriander leaves.

Serves 4

BASIC RECIPES

AIOLI

4 cloves Garlic Confit (page 160) or
   roasted garlic cloves
4 egg yolks
2 teaspoons Dijon mustard
2 teaspoons apple cider vinegar
2 tablespoons lemon juice
420 ml olive oil
sea salt and freshly ground black pepper

Place the garlic, egg yolks, mustard, vinegar
and lemon juice in a food processor and
whiz until combined. With the motor running,
slowly pour in the oil in a thin stream and
process until the aioli is thick and creamy.
Season with salt and pepper. Store in an
airtight container in the fridge for 4–5 days.

Makes 470 g

BARBECUE SAUCE

100 g tomato paste
3 tablespoons apple cider vinegar
2 tablespoons Dijon mustard
95 g honey
½ teaspoon smoked paprika
170 ml tamari
2 garlic cloves, crushed
pinch of ground cloves
pinch of ground cinnamon
sea salt and freshly ground black pepper

Place all the ingredients in a saucepan
over medium heat and bring to the boil.
Reduce the heat to low and simmer, stirring
occasionally, for 15 minutes until thickened.
Season with salt and pepper. Store in an
airtight container in the fridge for up to
2 weeks.

Makes 325 ml

BEEF BONE BROTH

about 2 kg beef knuckle and marrow
   bones
1 cow's foot, cut into pieces (optional)
3 tablespoons apple cider vinegar
1.5 kg meaty beef rib or neck bones
3 onions, roughly chopped
3 carrots, roughly chopped
3 celery stalks, roughly chopped
2 leeks, white part only, rinsed well
   and roughly chopped
3 thyme sprigs
2 bay leaves
1 teaspoon black peppercorns, crushed
1 garlic bulb, cut in half horizontally
2 large handfuls of flat-leaf parsley stalks

Place the knuckle and marrow bones and
cow's foot (if using) in a stockpot, add the
vinegar and 5 litres of cold water, or enough
to cover. Stand for 1 hour to draw out the
nutrients from the bones. Remove the bones
from the water, reserving the water.

Preheat the oven to 180°C.

Place the knuckle and marrow bones, cow's
foot (if using) and meaty bones in large tins
and roast in the oven for 30 minutes until
well browned. Add all the bones to the
stockpot or pan along with the vegetables.

Pour the fat out of the tins into a saucepan,
add 1 litre of the reserved water, place over
high heat and bring to a simmer, stirring with
a wooden spoon to loosen any coagulated
juices. Add this liquid to the bones and
vegetables.

Recipe continued over page >

BEEF BONE BROTH (CONT.)

Add additional reserved water to just cover the bones; the liquid should come no higher than 2 cm below the rim of the pan, as the volume will expand slightly during cooking.

Bring the broth to the boil, skimming off the scum that rises to the top. Reduce the heat to low and add the thyme, bay leaves, peppercorns and garlic. Simmer for 24–32 hours. Just before finishing, add the parsley and simmer for another 10 minutes. Strain the broth into a large container. Cover and refrigerate until the fat rises to the top and congeals. Skim off this fat and store the fat and the broth in separate airtight containers in the fridge or freezer. They can be stored in the fridge for 4 days or freezer for up to 3 months. The fat can be used for cooking meat, poultry or vegetable dishes.

Makes 3.5–4 litres

CAULIFLOWER RICE

1 head of cauliflower, florets and stalk roughly chopped
2 tablespoons coconut oil
sea salt and freshly ground black pepper

Place the cauliflower in a food processor and pulse into tiny pieces that look like rice.

Melt the coconut oil in a large frying pan over medium heat. Add the cauliflower and cook for 4–6 minutes, or until softened. Season with salt and pepper and serve.

Serves 4

CHICKEN BONE BROTH

1–1.5 kg bony chicken parts (necks, backs, breastbones and wings)
2–4 chicken feet (optional)
2 tablespoons apple cider vinegar
1 large onion, roughly chopped
2 carrots, roughly chopped
3 celery stalks, roughly chopped
2 leeks, white part only, rinsed well and roughly chopped
1 garlic bulb, cut in half horizontally
1 tablespoon black peppercorns, lightly crushed
2 bay leaves
2 large handfuls of flat-leaf parsley stalks

Place the chicken pieces in a stockpot, add 5 litres of cold water, the vinegar, onion, carrot, celery, leek, garlic, peppercorns and bay leaves and stand for 1 hour to draw out the nutrients from the bones.

Place the stockpot over medium–high heat and bring to the boil, skimming off the scum that rises to the top. Reduce the heat to low and simmer for 12–24 hours. The longer you cook the broth the richer and more flavourful it will be. About 10 minutes before the broth is ready, add the parsley.

Strain the broth through a fine sieve into a large storage container, cover and refrigerate until the fat rises to the top and congeals. Skim off this fat and store the fat and the broth in separate airtight containers in the fridge or freezer. They can be stored in the fridge for 4 days or freezer for up to 3 months. The fat can be used for cooking meat, poultry or vegetable dishes.

Makes 3.5 litres

CHILLI OIL

400 ml olive oil
4 tablespoons chilli flakes

Heat the oil in a saucepan over low heat. Add the chilli flakes and warm for 2 minutes. Do not boil. Remove from the heat and cool.

Store in a sealed glass jar or bottle in a cool, dark place. Shake the bottle every week or so. The longer you leave it, the hotter and redder the oil becomes.

Makes 400 ml

CRISPY SHALLOTS

250 ml (1 cup) coconut oil
4–8 French shallots, finely sliced

Melt the oil in a small saucepan over medium heat. Add the shallot and cook for 2–3 minutes until golden. Remove with a slotted spoon and drain on paper towel. (You can re-use the oil for sautéing vegetables or cooking meat, chicken or fish.)

Makes 2–4 tablespoons

COCONUT YOGHURT

flesh and water of 4 young coconuts*
juice of 2 lemons or limes
1–2 vanilla pods, split and seeds scraped
maple syrup or honey, to taste
2 probiotic capsules*

* See Glossary

Combine the coconut flesh, one-third of the coconut water, the lemon or lime juice, vanilla seeds and maple syrup or honey in a blender and blend until smooth. Add more coconut water to thin, if desired.

Open your probiotic capsules, pour into the blender and give one final quick whiz. Pour into a 1 litre sterilised glass jar, cover with paper towel and allow to sit for 6–12 hours at room temperature so that the bacteria can proliferate (break down the yoghurt). The longer you leave it, the tangier the yoghurt becomes. Store in the fridge in an airtight container for up to 2 weeks.

Makes 600 g

DUKKAH

40 g (¼ cup) pine nuts (activated if possible)
4 tablespoons coriander seeds
60 g white sesame seeds
¼ teaspoon ground cumin
¼ teaspoon sea salt
pinch of chilli powder
¼ teaspoon baharat*
pinch of dried mint

* See Glossary

Combine the pine nuts and coriander seeds in a large frying pan and toast over medium–high heat for 1 minute until the mixture has started to colour. Add the sesame seeds and toast for another minute until golden brown.

Pour the nut and seed mixture into the bowl of a food processor. Add the cumin, salt, chilli powder, baharat and mint and pulse to combine. Store in an airtight container in the pantry for 2–3 weeks.

Makes 110 g

NUT-FREE BREAD ROLLS

70 g (1 cup) psyllium husks*
70 g (½ cup) coconut flour, plus extra for dusting
3 tablespoons chia seeds
3 tablespoons flaxseeds
3 tablespoons pumpkin seeds
3 tablespoons white sesame seeds
3 tablespoons sunflower seeds
1 tablespoon coconut sugar or honey
2½ teaspoons baking powder
1½ teaspoons sea salt
1 tablespoon apple cider vinegar
3 eggs
2 tablespoons coconut oil, melted

See Glossary

Preheat the oven to 180°C. Line a baking tray with baking paper.

Place the psyllium husks, coconut flour, chia seeds, flaxseeds, pumpkin seeds, sesame seeds and sunflower seeds in the bowl of a food processor and whiz for a few seconds until the seeds are finely chopped.

Transfer the flour mixture to a large bowl, then mix in the coconut sugar or honey, baking powder and salt. In another bowl, combine the vinegar, 450 ml of water and the eggs and whisk until smooth. Add the coconut oil and egg mixture to the dry ingredients and mix to form a wet dough.

Knead the dough on a lightly floured work surface for 1 minute, then divide into six portions and roll into balls. Place the dough balls on the prepared tray, allowing room for spreading. Bake for 1 hour, rotating the tray halfway through so the rolls cook evenly. To check if they are cooked, tap the base of a roll. If it sounds hollow, the rolls are ready. If they seem to be very heavy and dense, they need to cook for a little longer. >

When the rolls are ready, pop them on a wire rack and leave them to cool completely, about 10–15 minutes. Serve straight away or store in the fridge for up to 1 week or the freezer for up to 3 months.

Makes 6

PALEO CHEESE

155 g (1 cup) cashew or macadamia nuts
375 ml (1½ cups) almond milk
4 tablespoons powdered gelatine
3 tablespoons lemon juice
1 teaspoon sea salt
pinch of freshly ground black pepper
3 tablespoons olive oil

Soak the cashew or macadamia nuts in 750 ml of water for 1–4 hours. Drain and rinse well.

Grease two 250 ml ramekins.

Bring the almond milk to a simmer in a saucepan, stir in the gelatine and mix until dissolved. Set aside, keeping warm until needed.

Place the cashew or macadamia nuts in the bowl of a food processor, add the lemon juice, salt and pepper and pulse for a minute to combine. Add 2 tablespoons of water and process until smooth. Pour in the almond milk mixture and olive oil and whiz until very smooth. Pass through a fine sieve, then spoon into the prepared ramekins. Cover with plastic wrap and place in the refrigerator for 2 hours to set. Keeps for up to 2 weeks in the fridge.

Makes 700 g

PALEO HOISIN SAUCE

juice of 1 orange
2 tablespoons almond butter
1 teaspoon grated garlic
1 tablespoon grated ginger
2 teaspoons apple cider vinegar
2 teaspoons honey
4 tablespoons tamari or coconut aminos*
½ teaspoon Chinese five spice
1½ teaspoons sesame oil
½ teaspoon chilli flakes or chilli powder
2 teaspoons tomato paste

* See Glossary

Place all the ingredients in a saucepan, add 2 tablespoons of water and bring to a simmer over medium–low heat. Cook, stirring constantly, for 5 minutes. Allow to cool, then blend until smooth. Store in an airtight container in the fridge for up to 1 week.

Makes 170 ml

PALEO ROTI BREAD

100 g (1 cup) almond meal
125 g (1 cup) tapioca flour*
125 ml (½ cup) coconut milk
sea salt
coconut oil, for cooking

* See Glossary

Combine the almond meal, tapioca flour, coconut milk and 125 ml of water in a bowl, mix well and season with salt.

Heat a small non-stick frying pan over medium heat. Add enough oil to coat the surface of the pan, then pour in 3 tablespoons of batter and swirl around slightly. Cook for 2½ minutes until mostly cooked through, then flip and cook for 3 minutes until golden and crisp. Repeat with the remaining mixture. Store the rotis in the fridge for up to 1 week or freeze for up to 3 months.

Makes 6

SAUERKRAUT WITH DILL & JUNIPER BERRIES

1 star anise
1 teaspoon whole cloves
600 g cabbage (savoy or red, or
  a mixture of the two)
1½ teaspoons sea salt
3 tablespoons chopped dill
2 tablespoons juniper berries (see note)
1 sachet vegetable starter culture (this will
  weigh 2–5 g, depending on the brand,
  see note)
1 handful of dill fronds, to serve

You will need a 1.5 litre preserving jar with an airlock lid for this recipe. Wash the jar and all the utensils you will be using in very hot water or run them through a hot rinse cycle in the dishwasher.

Place the star anise and cloves in a small piece of muslin, tie into a bundle and set aside. Remove the outer leaves of the cabbage. Choose one of the outer leaves, wash it well and set aside. Shred the cabbage in a food processor, slice by hand or use a mandoline, then place in a large glass or stainless steel bowl. Sprinkle on the salt, dill and juniper berries, mix well, cover with plastic wrap and set aside while you prepare the starter culture.

Dissolve the starter culture in water according to the packet instructions (the amount of water needed will depend on the brand you are using). Add to the cabbage along with the muslin bag containing the spices and mix well. >

Fill the prepared jar with the cabbage mixture, pressing down well with a large spoon or potato masher to remove any air pockets and leaving 2 cm of room free at the top. The cabbage should be completely submerged in the liquid; add more water if necessary.

Take the clean cabbage leaf, fold it up and place it on top of the cabbage mixture, then add a small glass weight (a shot glass is ideal) to keep everything submerged. Close the lid, then wrap a tea towel around the side of the jar to block out the light. Store in a dark place with a temperature of 16–23°C for 10–14 days. (Place the jar in an esky to maintain a more consistent temperature.) Different vegetables have different culturing times and the warmer it is, the shorter the time needed. The longer you leave the jar, the higher the level of good bacteria present and the tangier the flavour.

Chill before eating. Once opened, mix through the dill tips and serve. The sauerkraut will last for up to 2 months in the fridge when kept submerged in the liquid. If unopened, it will keep for up to 9 months in the fridge.

Makes 1 x 1.5 litre jar

NOTES

Juniper berries can be found at some health food stores, specialty food stores or online.

Vegetable starter culture is used to kick-start the fermentation process when culturing veggies and is available from health food stores or online.

NOM NOM'S SRIRACHA CHILLI SAUCE

680 g long red chillies or red jalapeno chillies, deseeded and roughly chopped
8 garlic cloves, crushed
4 tablespoons apple cider vinegar
3 tablespoons tomato paste
1 large medjool date, pitted
2 tablespoons fish sauce
1½ teaspoons sea salt

Combine all the ingredients in a food processor and process until smooth. Pour into a saucepan and bring to the boil over high heat, stirring occasionally. Reduce the heat to low and simmer, stirring now and then, for 5–10 minutes until vibrant and red. Remove from the heat and cool. Transfer to a large glass jar and refrigerate for up to 2 weeks.

Makes 625 g

TAHINI & YOGHURT DRESSING

3 tablespoons hulled tahini
3 tablespoons coconut yoghurt (for a recipe, see page 159)
2 tablespoons lemon juice
1 garlic clove, finely chopped
2 pinches of sumac, to serve
sea salt and freshly ground black pepper

Mix all the ingredients in a small bowl with 3 tablespoons of water. Store in an airtight container in the fridge for up to 2 weeks.

Makes about 140 g

TURKISH SPICE MIX

35 g (⅓ cup) ground cumin
3 tablespoons dried mint
3 tablespoons dried oregano
2 tablespoons sweet paprika
2 tablespoons freshly ground black pepper
2 teaspoons hot paprika

Combine all the ingredients in a bowl and mix well. Store in an airtight container in the pantry for up to 6 months.

Makes 75 g

WORCESTERSHIRE SAUCE

125 ml (½ cup) apple cider vinegar
2½ tablespoons coconut aminos* or tamari
½ teaspoon ground ginger
½ teaspoon mustard powder
½ teaspoon onion powder
½ teaspoon garlic powder
¼ teaspoon ground cinnamon
¼ teaspoon freshly ground black pepper
* See Glossary

Combine all the ingredients with 2 tablespoons of water in a saucepan and, stirring occasionally, bring to the boil over medium heat. Turn down the heat to low and simmer for 10 minutes. Remove from the heat and allow to cool. Pour into a sterilised bottle and store in the fridge for up to 1 month.

Makes 125 ml

GLOSSARY

ACTIVATED NUTS AND SEEDS

Nuts and seeds are a great source of healthy fats, but they contain phytic acid, which binds to minerals such as iron, zinc, calcium, potassium and magnesium so that they can't be readily absorbed. Activating nuts and seeds lessens the phytates, making sure that we absorb as many of the good things as possible. Activated nuts and seeds are available from health food stores. Or to save money and make your own, simply soak the nuts in filtered water (hard nuts, like almonds, need to soak for 12 hours; softer nuts, like cashews and macadamias, only need 4–6 hours). Rinse the nuts well under running water, then spread out on a baking tray and place in a 50°C oven or dehydrator to dry out. This will take anywhere from 6 to 24 hours, depending on the temperature and the kind of nuts or seeds you are using. Store in an airtight container in the pantry for up to 3 months.

ARROWROOT

Arrowroot is a starch made from the roots of several tropical plants. In Australia, arrowroot and tapioca flour are considered to be the same thing, even though they actually come from different plants. Arrowroot is gluten free and is often used in baking and to thicken sauces and to can be found at health food stores and some supermarkets. *See also* Tapioca Flour.

BAHARAT

Baharat is a Middle Eastern spice blend that usually includes black pepper, coriander, paprika, cardamom, nutmeg, cumin, cloves and cinnamon. Baharat is great for seasoning meats and vegetables, adding to dips and sauces, or using as a dry rub or marinade for veggies, meat and fish. Look for baharat at Middle Eastern grocers and delis.

BARBERRIES

Barberries are the fruit of the thorny berberis shrub and are mainly used in Mediterranean and Middle Eastern cuisines. The small, sour, ruby red berries are rich in zinc and vitamin B and C. They have a tart, lemony flavour making them great for meats, salads and couscous dishes. Barberries can either be used in their dried form or rehydrated. Barberries can be found at Middle Eastern grocers.

BONITO FLAKES

Bonito flakes are made from the bonito fish, which is like a small tuna. The fish is smoked, fermented, dried and shaved, and the end product looks similar to wood shavings. Bonito flakes are used to garnish Japanese dishes, to make sauces such as ponzu, soups such as miso and to make the Japanese stock, dashi. You can find bonito flakes in Asian food stores.

CASSIA BARK

Cassia bark is a type of cinnamon that originates from southern China and is cultivated throughout South East Asia. Cassia is the most common type of cinnamon found on supermarket shelves and varies from Ceylon or 'true' cinnamon in a number of ways. Quills from cassia bark are thick and not easily broken, while Ceylon cinnamon sticks have thin, fibrous layers. Cassia also has a stronger and spicier taste. Both cassia and Ceylon cinnamon have been used medicinally for thousands of years to treat colds, arthritis, high blood pressure and abdominal pain.

CHIPOTLE CHILLIES IN ADOBO SAUCE

Chipotle chillies are smoke-dried jalapenos and are commonly used in Mexican cooking. They impart a mild but earthy spiciness to dishes and are delicious when pureed and mixed through homemade aioli. They are often sold in jars or tins immersed in adobo sauce – a type of sauce or marinade widely used in Latin American cuisine, usually made from tomatoes, onions, chillies, garlic, vinegar and spices. You can also buy chipotle chillies in dried, powdered form. Look for them at Central and South American food stores, as well as some gourmet food stores.

COCONUT AMINOS

Coconut aminos is made from the raw sap of the coconut tree, which is naturally aged and blended with sea salt. It is a great alternative to soy sauce as it has a higher amino acid content and no gluten. It is also slightly less salty than tamari. You'll find coconut aminos in health food stores.

GOOD-QUALITY ANIMAL FAT

I use either coconut oil or good-quality animal fats for cooking as they have high smoke points (meaning they do not oxidise at high temperatures). Some of my favourite animal fats to use are lard (pork fat), tallow (rendered beef fat), rendered chicken fat and duck fat. These may be hard to find – ask at your local butcher or meat supplier, or you can also look online for meat suppliers who sell them.

KELP NOODLES

Kelp noodles are clear noodles made from seaweed. They contain more than 70 nutrients and minerals, including iron, potassium, magnesium, calcium, iodine and more than 21 amino acids. Kelp noodles are great for stir-fries, casseroles, soups and salads. You can find them at health food stores.

KOMBU

Kombu is a high-protein sea vegetable, rich in calcium, iron, iodine and dietary fibre. It is salty and savoury and plays a vital role in Japanese cuisine. Kombu can be used in a similar way to bay leaves – add a few pieces to a stew or curry for a flavour boost and remove them after cooking. Kombu can be found in Asian grocers and is mainly sold dried or pickled in vinegar. Dried kombu is often covered with a white powder from natural salts and starch. It is harmless but can easily be removed with a damp cloth.

NORI SHEETS

Nori is a dark green, paper-like, toasted seaweed used for most kinds of sushi and other Japanese dishes. Nori provides an abundance of essential nutrients and is rich in vitamins, iron, minerals, amino acids, omega-3 and omega-6, and antioxidants. Nori sheets are commonly used to roll sushi, but they can also be added to salads, soups, and fish, meat and vegetable dishes. You can buy nori sheets from Asian grocers and most supermarkets.

PROBIOTIC CAPSULES

Probiotic capsules contain live bacteria that can help to regulate digestion, clear up yeast infections and assist with conditions such as irritable bowel syndrome. These capsules need to be kept in the fridge. They can be swallowed whole, or opened up and used to ferment drinks such as kefir. Probiotic capsules can be found at pharmacies and health food stores.

PSYLLIUM HUSKS

Psyllium is a gluten-free, light brown soluble fibre produced from the *Plantago ovata* plant, native to India and Pakistan. Psyllium is an indigestible dietary fibre, and is primarily used to maintain intestinal health, as the high fibre content absorbs excess liquid in the gut. When exposed to liquids, the husks swell up to create a gel. It is therefore important to drink plenty of fluids when consuming psyllium. Psyllium products can be found at health food stores and some supermarkets.

SHICHIMI TOGARASHI

Shichimi togarashi literally means 'seven flavour chilli pepper' and is one of the most popular condiments on Japanese tables. As the name suggests, this spice mixture is made from seven ingredients, typically shichimi togarashi includes red chilli, Japanese (sansho) peppers, orange peel, black and white sesame seeds, ginger and seaweed. The chillies aside, the ingredients vary, and if you are lucky you may come across a Japanese vendor offering a custom blend.

SHISO LEAVES

Shiso leaves, also known as perilla, are commonly used in Japanese cuisine. There are red, purple and green varieties of shiso and they are used in many ways – finely sliced on top of noodle dishes, chopped and added to batters, or scattered over any number of dishes as a garnish. Shiso has quite a pungent, grassy flavour that is lost when it is cooked for a long time. You can find shiso leaves at Asian grocers.

TAPIOCA FLOUR

Tapioca flour is made by grinding up the dried root of the manioc (cassava) plant. It can be used to thicken dishes or in gluten-free baking. You can find tapioca flour at health food stores and some supermarkets. *See also* Arrowroot.

WAKAME

Wakame is an edible seaweed commonly used in Japanese, Korean and Chinese cuisine. It is great in soups, salads and stir-fries. Wakame contains iron, magnesium, iodine, calcium and lignans. You can find it in Asian grocers and some supermarkets.

YOUNG COCONUTS

Young coconuts are harvested at 5–7 months and are usually white in colour. The best way to open one is to cut a circle in the top using a large knife and then prise this circle off. The amount of coconut water inside varies, but is usually around 250 ml. It is a good source of potassium and makes a refreshing drink on a hot day. Once you've poured the water out of the coconut, you can scoop out the soft flesh using a spoon. Look for young coconuts at Asian grocers and health food stores.

YUZU JUICE

Yuzu is a Japanese citrus fruit that has an extraordinary spicy citrus flavour, somewhere between a lemon and a lime. Yuzu juice is very high in vitamin C and is great in cocktails, dressings, dips and sashimi dishes. You can buy yuzu juice from Asian grocers.

Thank you to my beautiful partner in life and love, Nicola. I am seriously the luckiest bloke on the planet. Thank you for nurturing me and the little bunnies, Indii and Chilli, with love and food. I love you!

To my bunnies, Indii and Chilli – you know this book wouldn't have come about if it weren't for you. I love you both so much and you are both so unique in your own special ways. I hope that by the time your own children are at school this way of living will be considered normal and the current dietary guidelines considered extreme.

To Mark Roper (photography) and Deb Kaloper (styling) – thanks for once again making my food shine brightly!

To Steve Brown (photography) and Lucy Tweed (styling) – thanks for the extra lifestyle images for the book and the brilliant cover shots.

To Mary Small and Jane Winning – once again, it was a pleasure working with you and creating another much-needed book.

To Megan Johnston – thank you for your careful and thorough editing.

To Kirby Armstrong – thanks again for creating another fabulous design for the book.

To Monica and Jacinta Cannataci – girls, I can't thank you enough, and I am so happy that you have discovered that food really is medicine. You are the doctors of the future.

To Charlotte Ree – thanks for being the best publicist any author could wish to work with.

To Mum – thanks for passing on your love of cooking.

And finally to my mentors and the trailblazers in health and nutrition, I couldn't have done it without you: Nora Gedgaudas and Lisa Collins, Dr Libby, Trevor Hendy, Luke Hines, Helen Padarin, Pete Melov, Rudy Eckhardt, Pete Bablis, William (Bill) Davis, Tim Noakes, Gary Fettke, David Perlmutter, Gary Taubes, Frank Lipman, Wes and Charlotte Carr, Nahko Bear, Michael Franti, Trevor Hall, David Gillespie, Ben Balzer, Loren Cordain, Bruce Fife, Mat Lalonde, Martha Herbert, Joseph Mercola, Sally Fallon, Dr Natasha Campbell-McBride, Kitsa Yanniotis and Donna Gates.

Cook with Love & Laughter,
Pete Evans

INDEX

A PLUM BOOK

First published in 2016 by
Pan Macmillan Australia Pty Limited
Level 25, 1 Market Street,
Sydney, NSW 2000, Australia

Level 1, 15–19 Claremont Street,
South Yarra, Victoria 3141, Australia

Text copyright © Pete Evans 2016
Photographs copyright © Mark Roper 2016 except images on pages 2, 4,
7, 9, 10, 20, 21, 34, 35, 56, 57, 82, 83, 106, 107, 128, 129, 166,
170 and 176 © Steve Brown 2016

Design by Kirby Armstrong
Photography by Mark Roper (with additional photography by Steve Brown)
Prop and food styling by Deb Kaloper (with additional styling by Lucy Tweed)
Edited by Megan Johnston
Typeset by Pauline Haas
Index by Jo Rudd
Colour reproduction by Splitting Image Colour Studio
Printed and bound in China by 1010 Printing International Limited

A CIP catalogue record for this book is available from the National Library of Australia.

The publisher would like to thank The Academy Brand for their generosity in providing
clothing for the book.

1 0 9 8 7 6 5